FANTASTIC PLACES TO FART IN CANADA

COLORING BOOK

BY BRANDON BISHOP

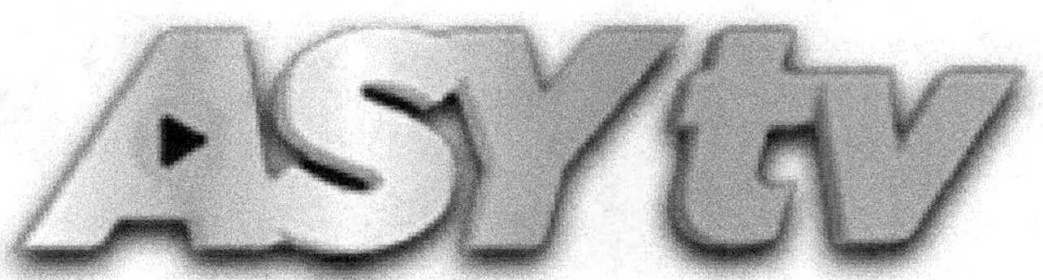

Fantastic Places to Fart in Canada Coloring Book
Written and Illustrated by Brandon Bishop

Published by Burning Bulb Publishing, P.O. Box 4721, Bridgeport, WV 26330
ISBN: 978-1-948278-99-7

FANTASTIC PLACES TO FART IN CANADA

A Coloring Book by Brandon Bishop

"O Canada!" A Place I Love to Fart! Yeah! That's Right Canucks! It's going down in The Great White North! For centuries, Canada has gotten off lightly as our upstairs neighbors, but now we bring the steam and we're gonna wilt some Maple Leaves!

So get out to Canada colors ready, grab a Molson Ice, fix up a stack of flapjacks and let's crack a rat all over Canada!

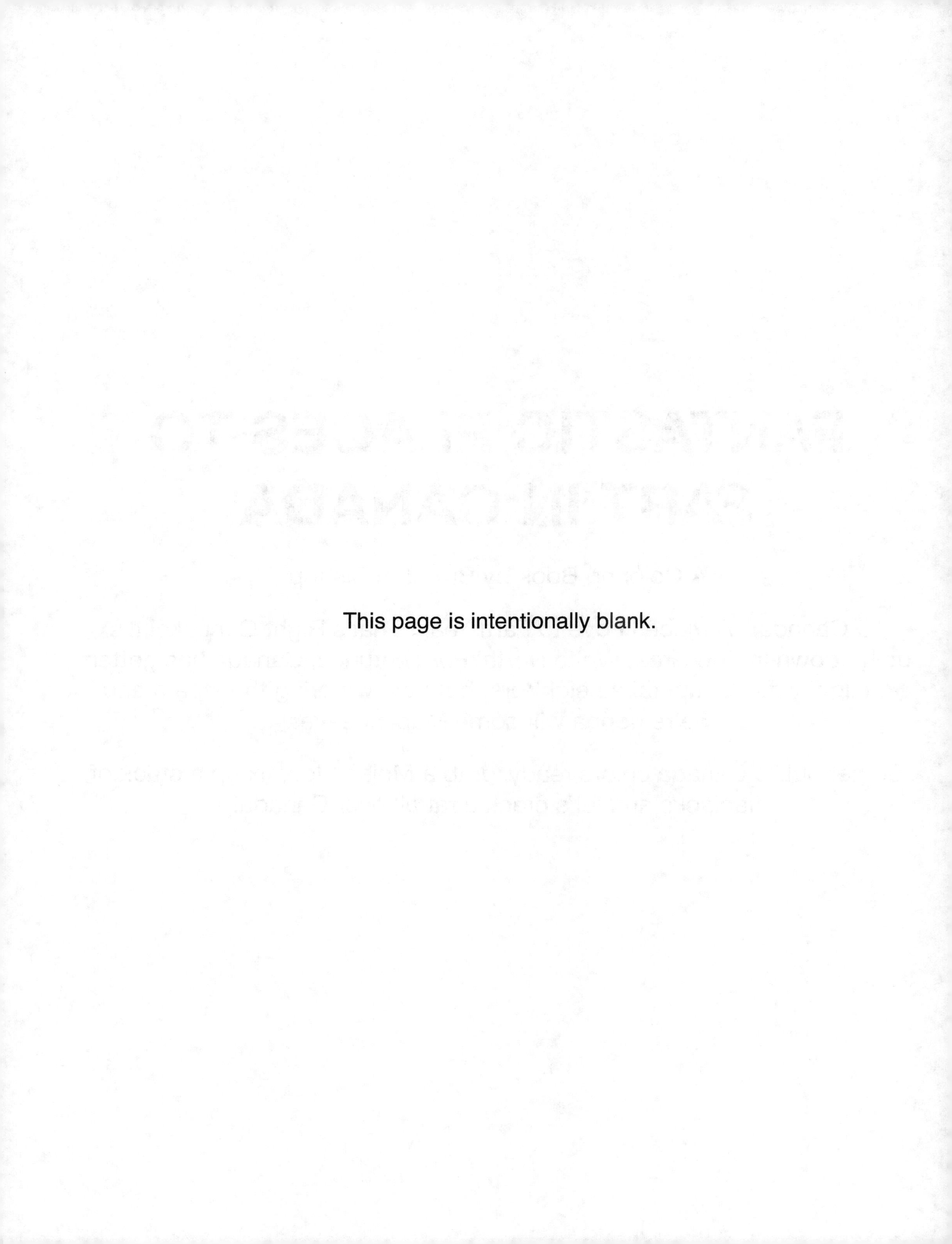
This page is intentionally blank.

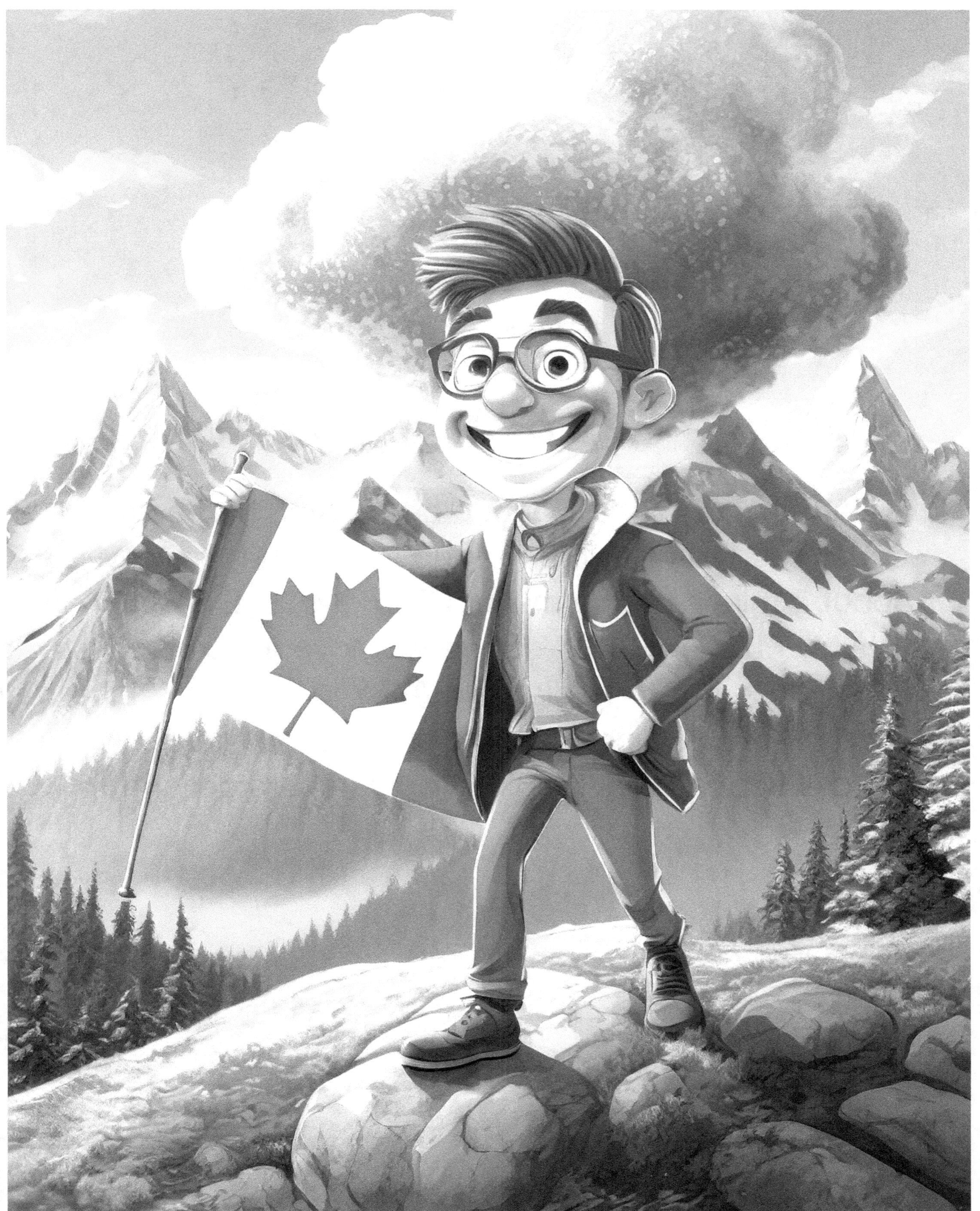

FRAAAAPJACKS?

Before your trip to Canada begins you had best get accustomed to what they eat up there. They have MAYBE about 5 things on the menu, BEER, MAPLE SYRUP and certainly FLAPJACKS! Yes, we ALL love a nice fluffy stack of pancakes, but Canadians REALLY love them… Like way too much… So grab a plate and then let go of a very pleasant aroma. Maple syrup farts are delightful.

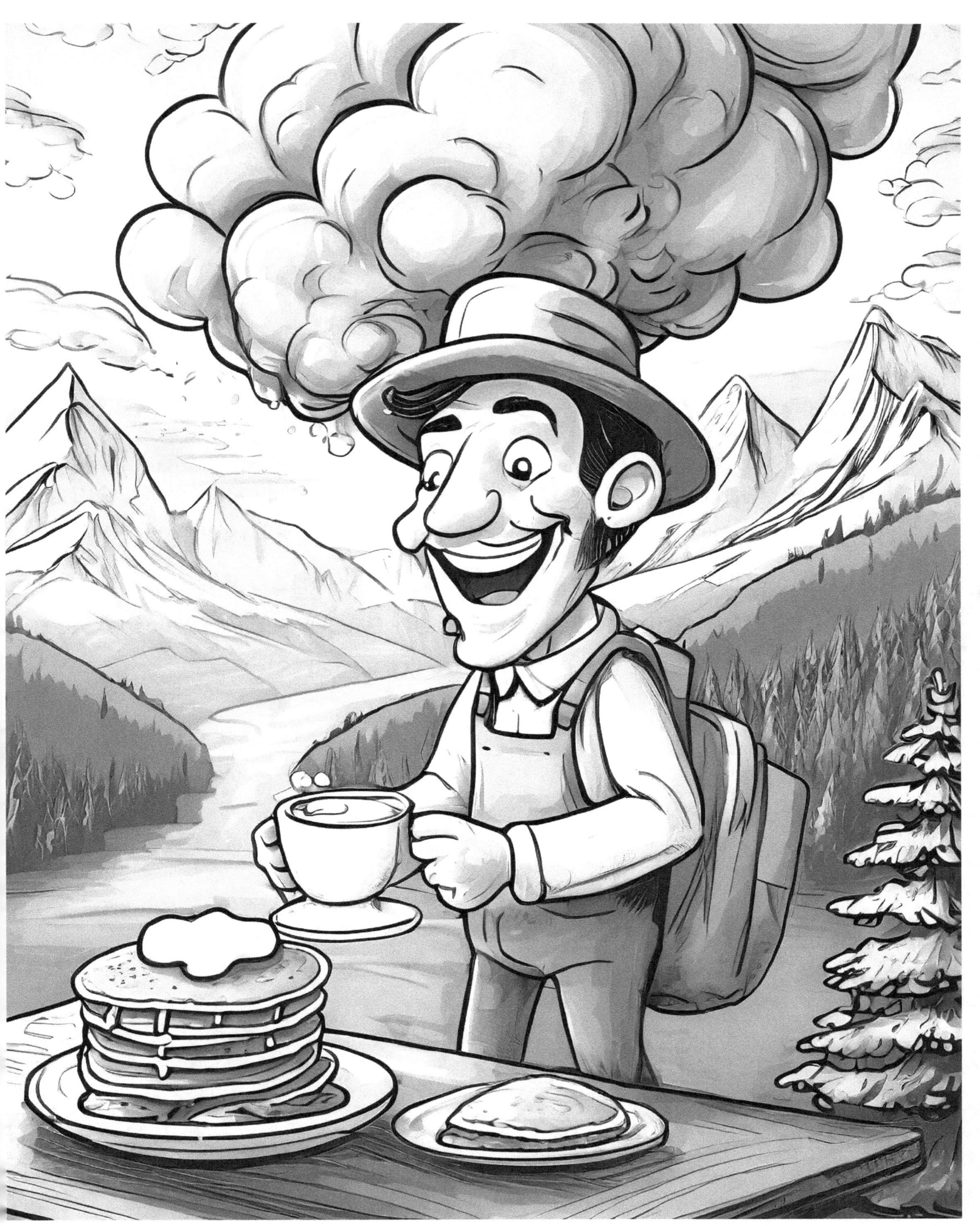

HOCKEY FARTS IN CANADA!

You better learn to pass the puck before you hit the ice and pass some gas! If you're not a fan of this chilly sport in Canada, you WILL BE HUNTED DOWN! So whether you love it or not, get those skates on and MELT SOME ICE with your heat seeking farts!

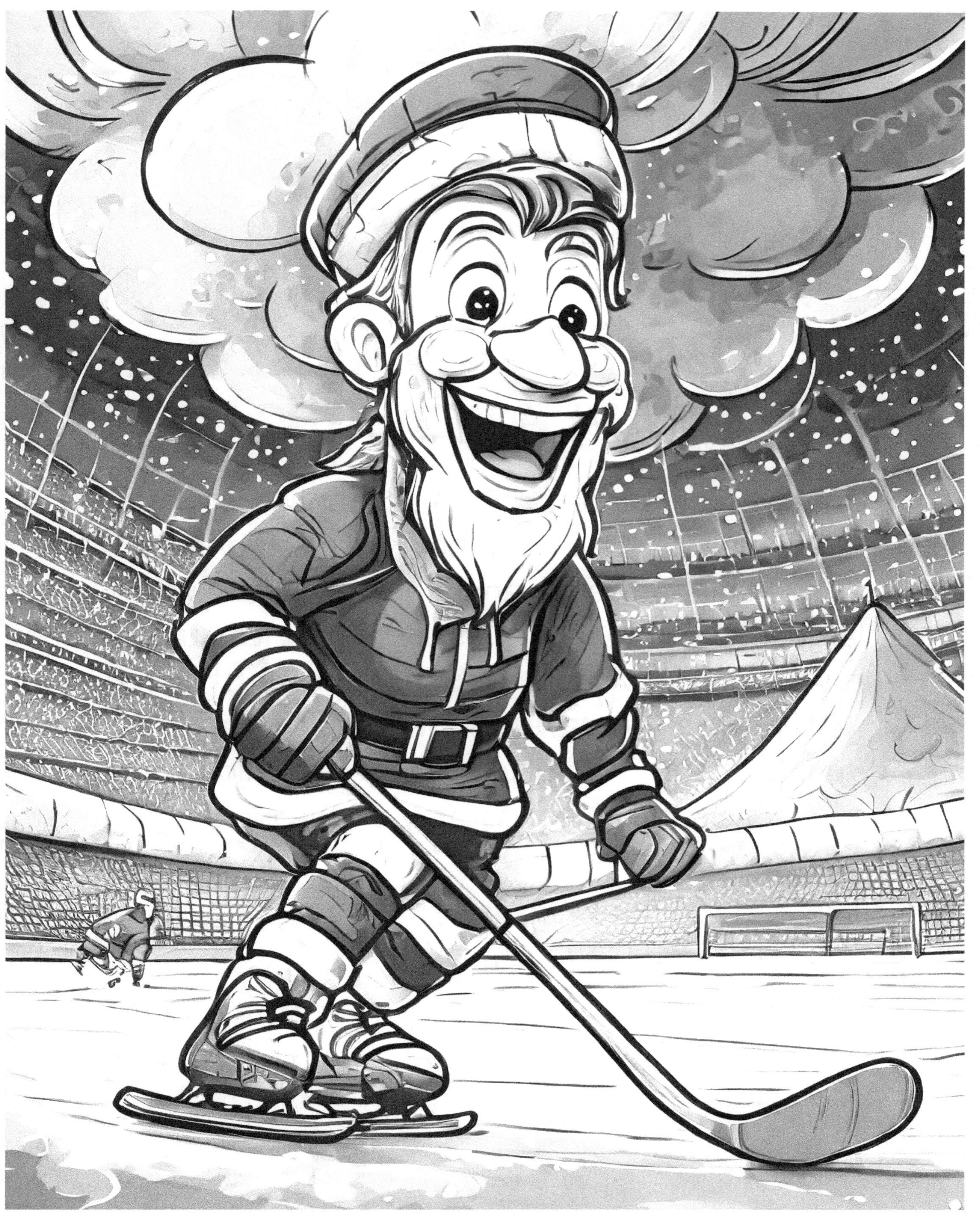

WHAT'S WITH ALL OF MAPLE LEAVES?

Once you cross the border into Canada or get off the plane, you will be showered with gifts of maple leaf necklaces and a hockey jersey with a large maple leaf on it... It's weird, but it's custom to welcome all visitors in this manner. Just accept it with a smile, take a shot of the customary maple syrup once given to you and enjoy your stay in the nicest country on the planet.

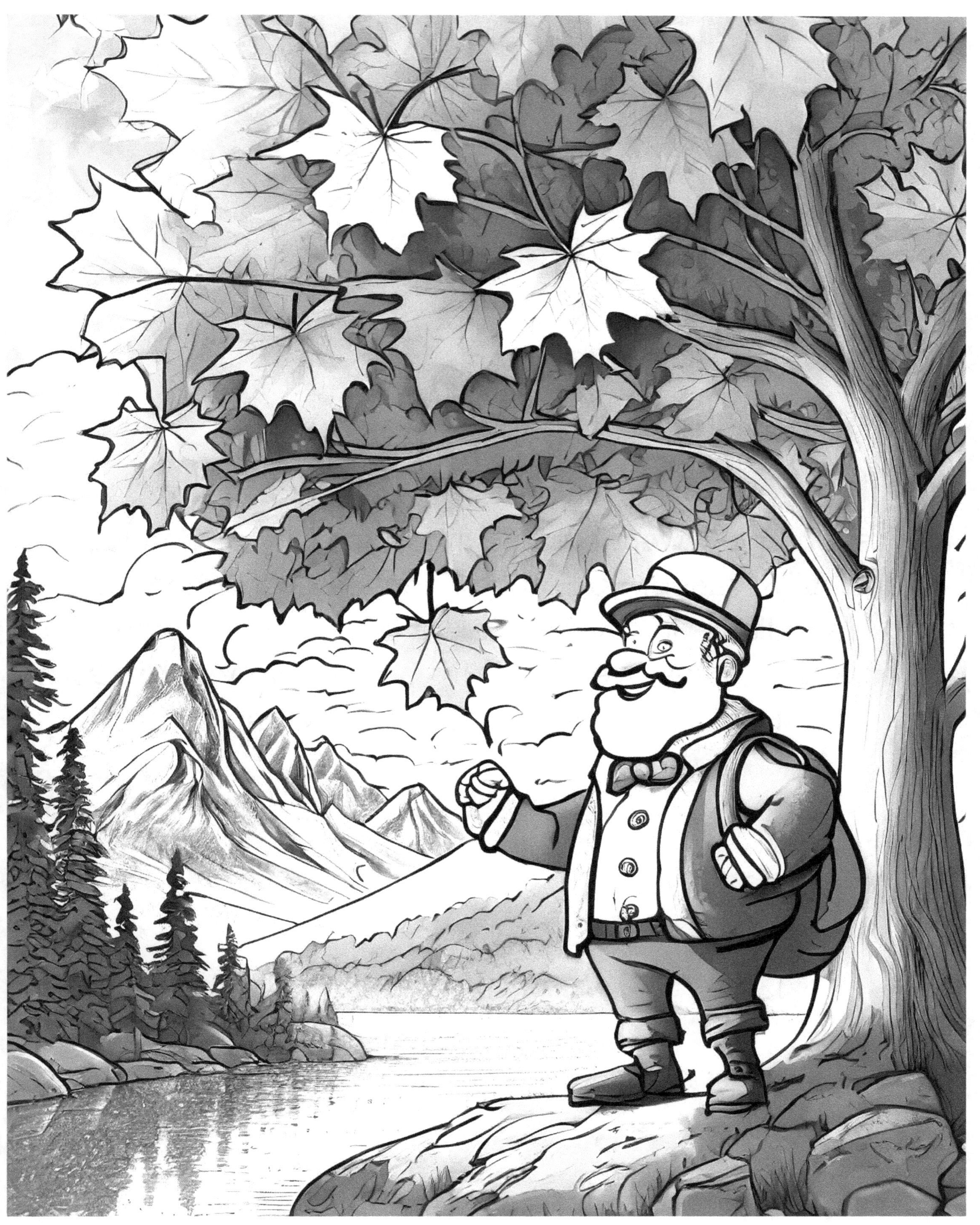

GRAVY ON FRIES?

"French Fries" were created in France. 1/4 of Canada is basically France. So French Fries are everywhere. But Canadians do a little bit extra by pouring copious amounts of gravy over them. It's actually very good, as is Poutine… Great fart source material…

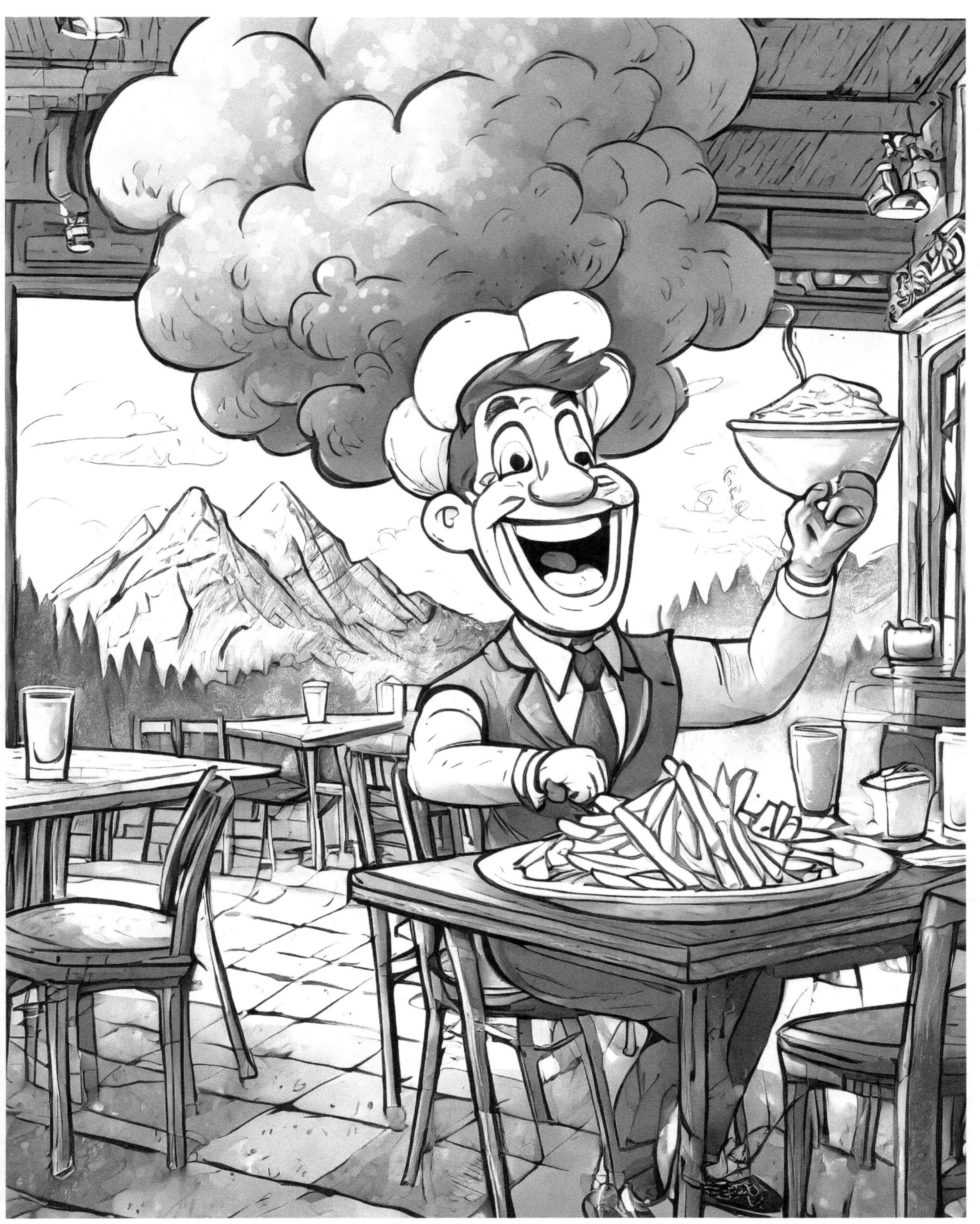

PASS WIND ON A MOOSE!

As a right of passage for growing boys in Canada, it is customary to squeeze out a bugle buster on a living breathing moose in the wild. I don't know when this tradition started, but it's a very real thing that boys accomplish before becoming fully grown Canadian men. Try it… And PLEASE video tape the whole thing.

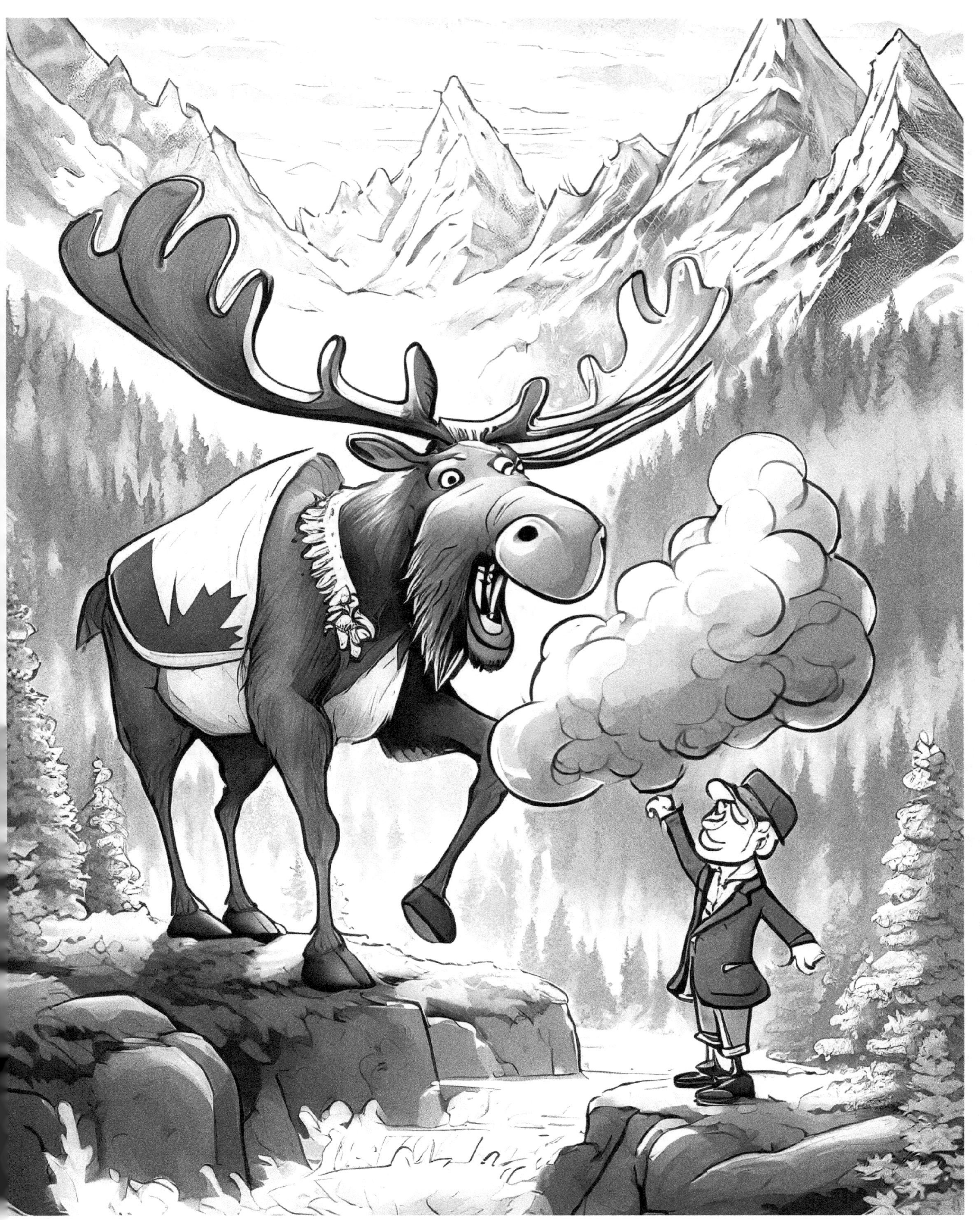

BEER FARTS!

Yes, Canadian Beer is more potent… Yes, You only have to be 19 to drink. Yes, the strip clubs are fully nude… Well, they we're… Is that still a thing? But back to beer… On your Canadian trip, do as the Canadians. Watch old reruns of SCTV and drink a Canadian beer. Oh… And wear Santa Claus hats… Most Canadians wear them 24/7.

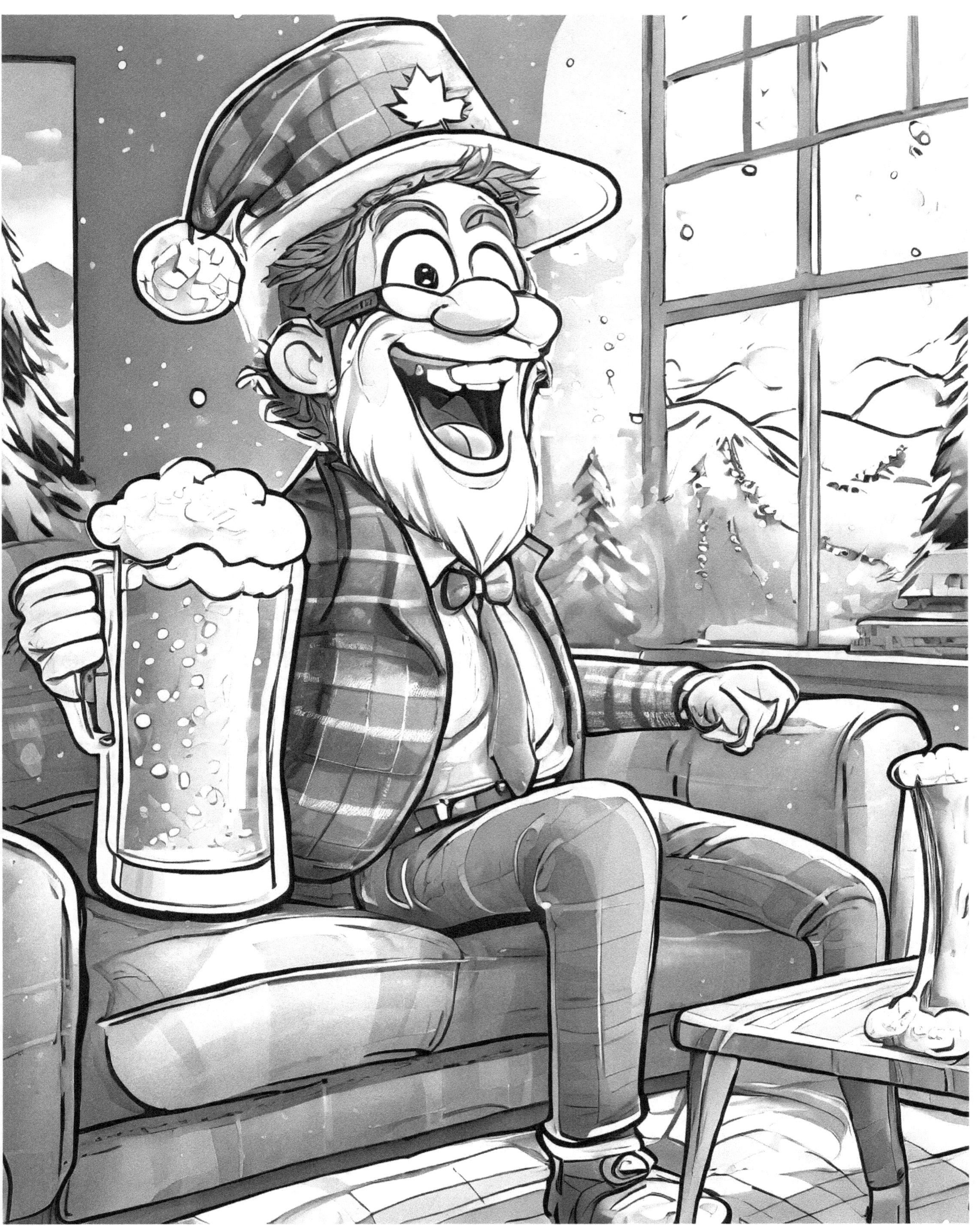

Canadian Music…

If the sounds of your own farts are driving you batty, drown out the thunder from down under with some soothing tunes by Alan's Morrisette, Bryan Adams, Barenaked Ladies, KD Lang, Anne Murray and Celine Dion… Those are the ONLY artists Canada permits anyone to listen to. So don't be bringing any of that rap or country garbage across to border.

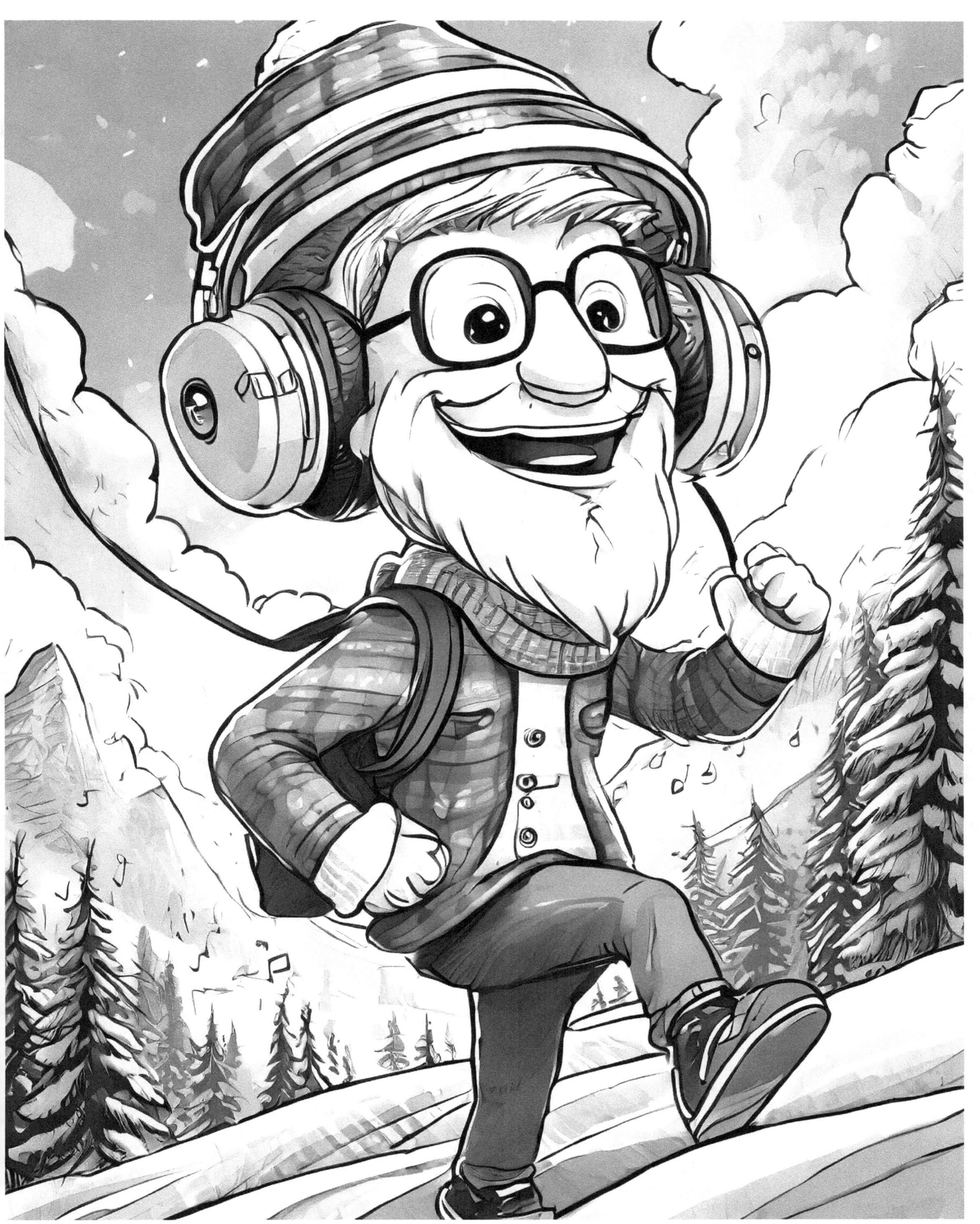

FARTING IN A PARK IN TORONTO

I don't know what it is, But Toronto is awesome! And Farting in Toronto is just the best. I highly recommend!

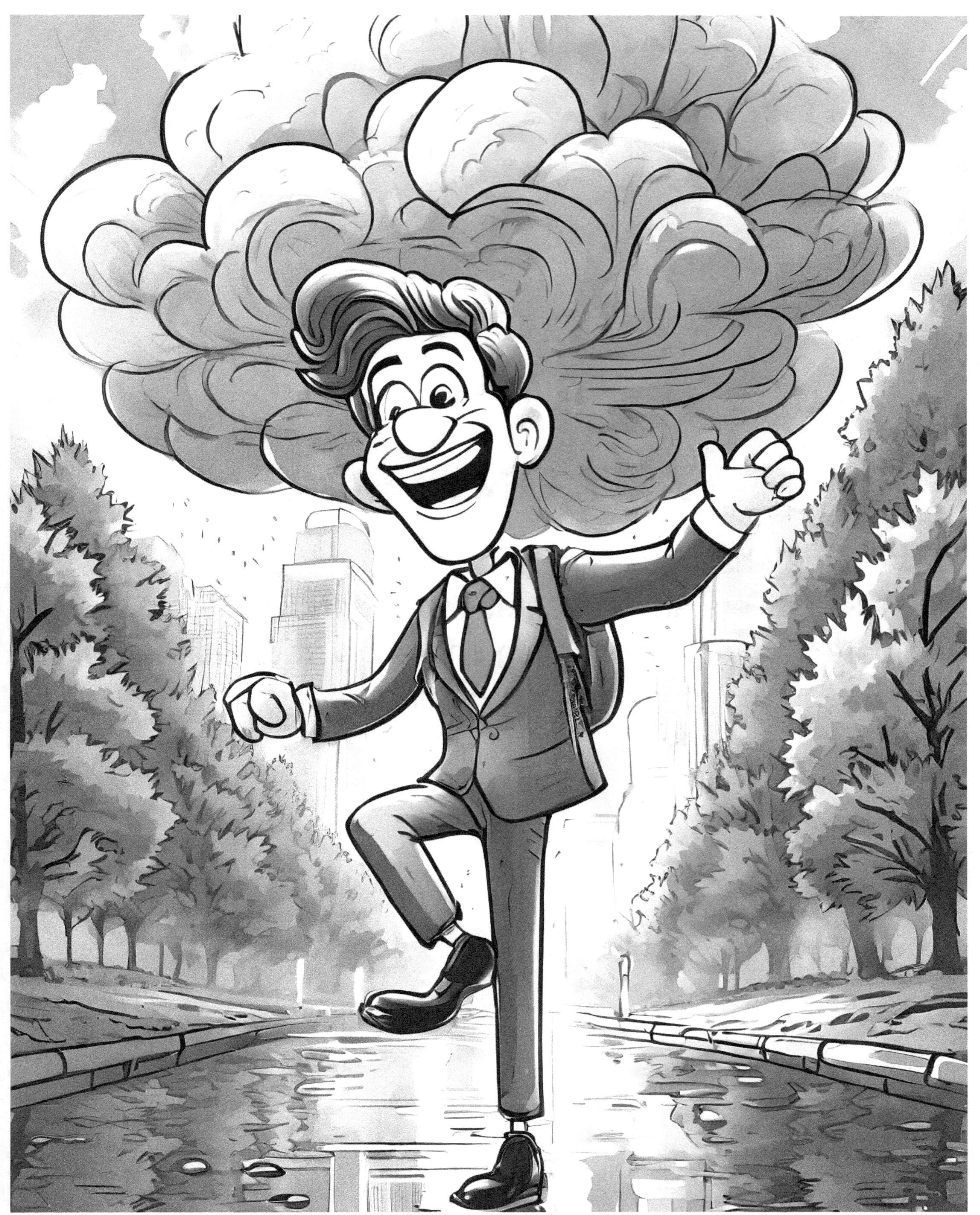

FART ON A BOAT

Canada has over 7 million one hundred and twelve lakes, rivers and streams. You simply MUST grab a boat, grab a Canadian flag and show your love for this amazing place. Bring beer…

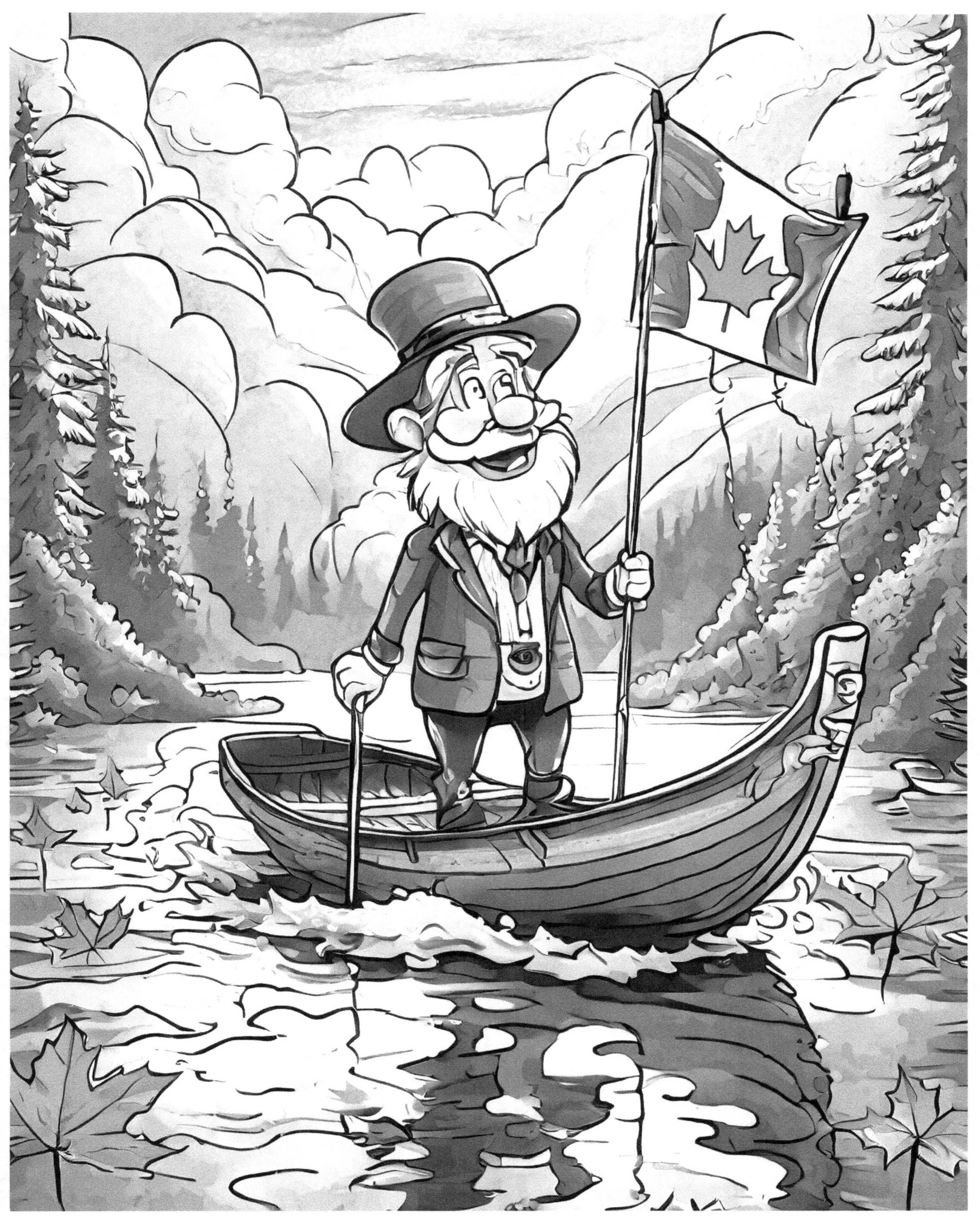

DOES A BEAR FART IN THE WOODS?

Yes…

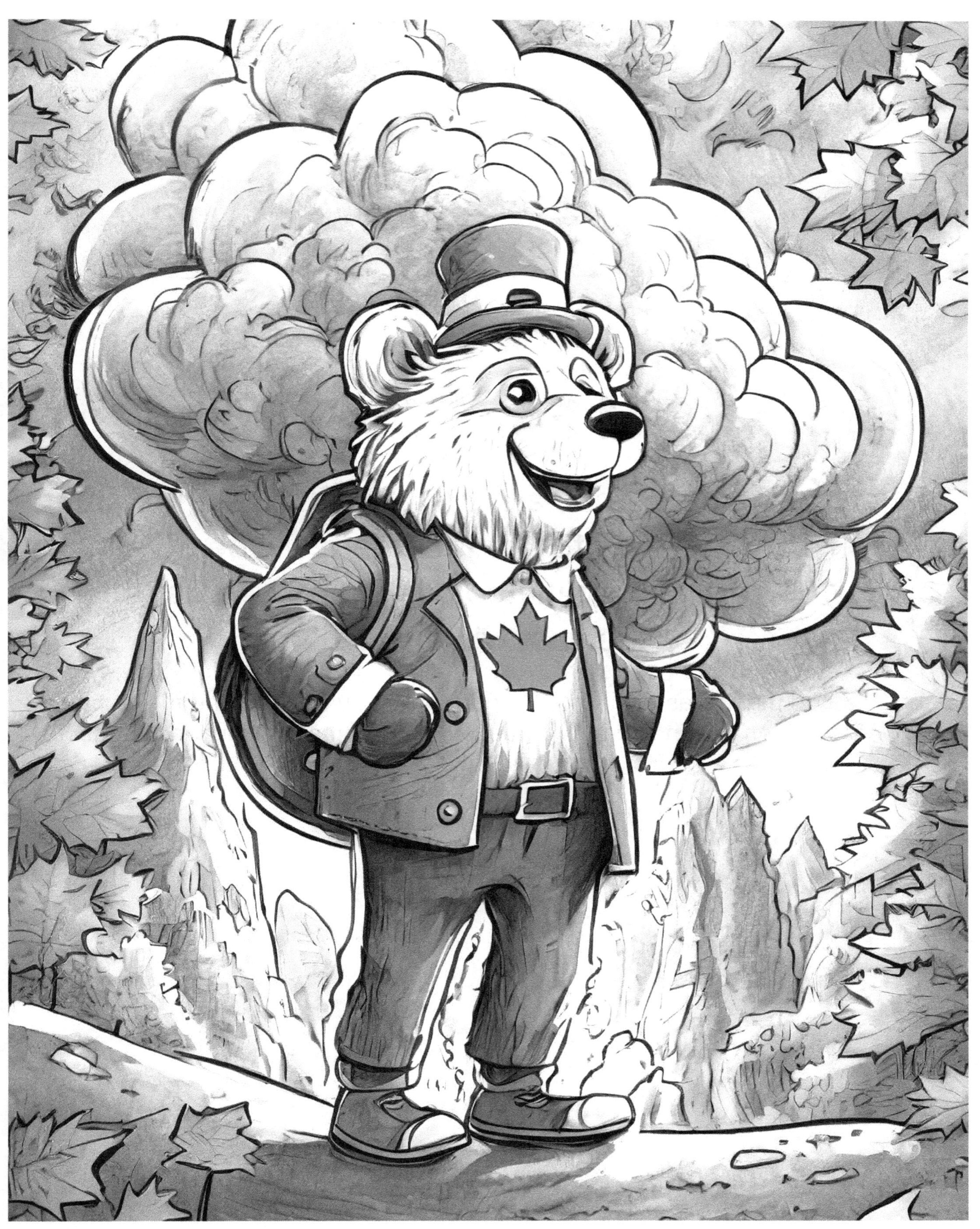

TIM FARTON'S!

Yeah, it's true. Canadians are OBSESSED with Tim Horton's. It was put into law that there will be a Timmy's every 100 yards in populated cities, and one per mile in the vast wilderness.

(Once I found that it was owned by Burger King, I shy'd away. And the two times I went to an American Timmy's it was terrible. But maybe Canada is better.)

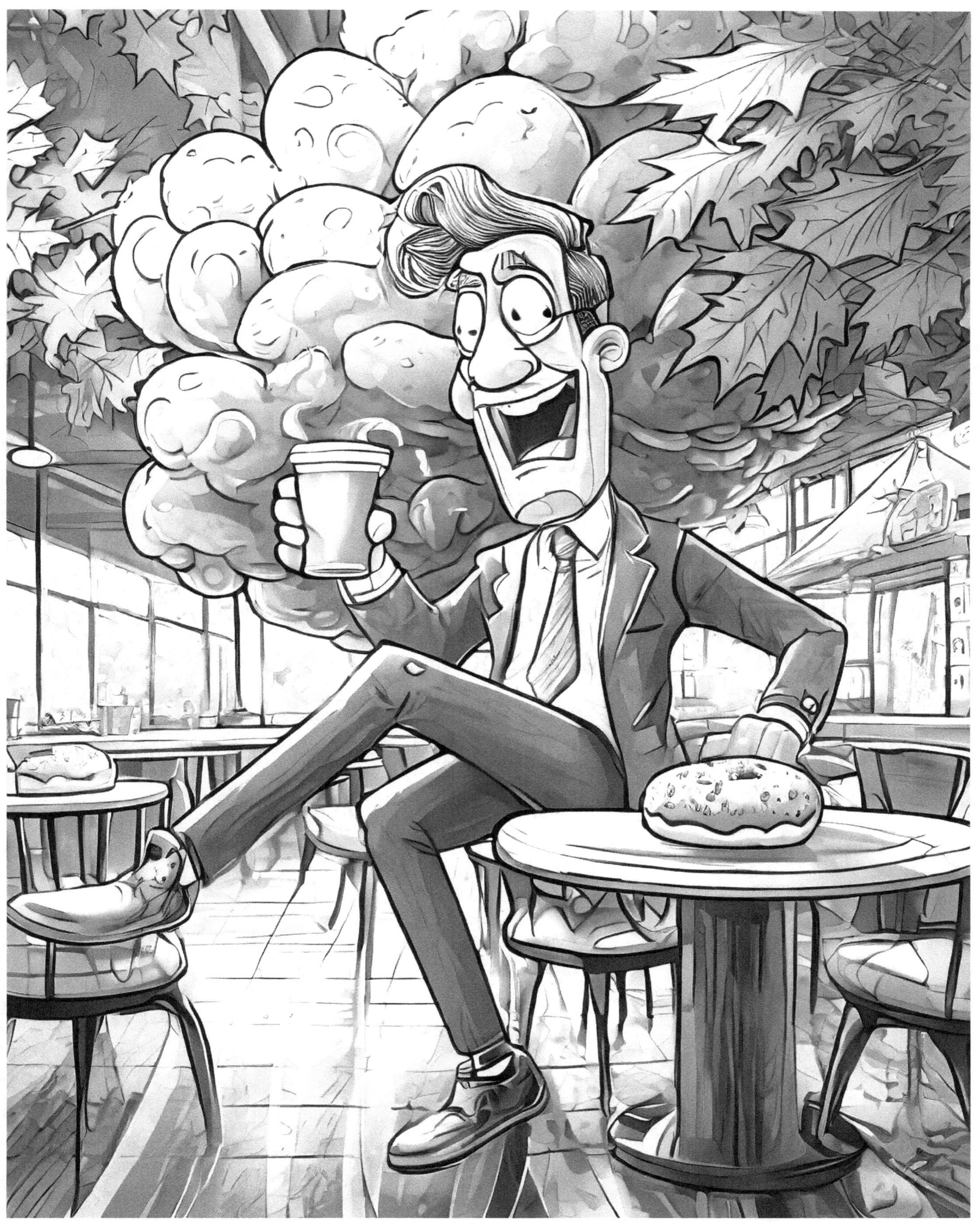

THE NICEST PEOPLE ON EARTH!

If your cars breaks down in Canada, someone will stop what they're doing and fix it for free within 20 minutes. That's just what they do and how they are in Canada. Even if you belt out your loudest most aggressive angry Cheek Buckler, they're probably apologize to you for getting in its path. "Sorry…Eh?"

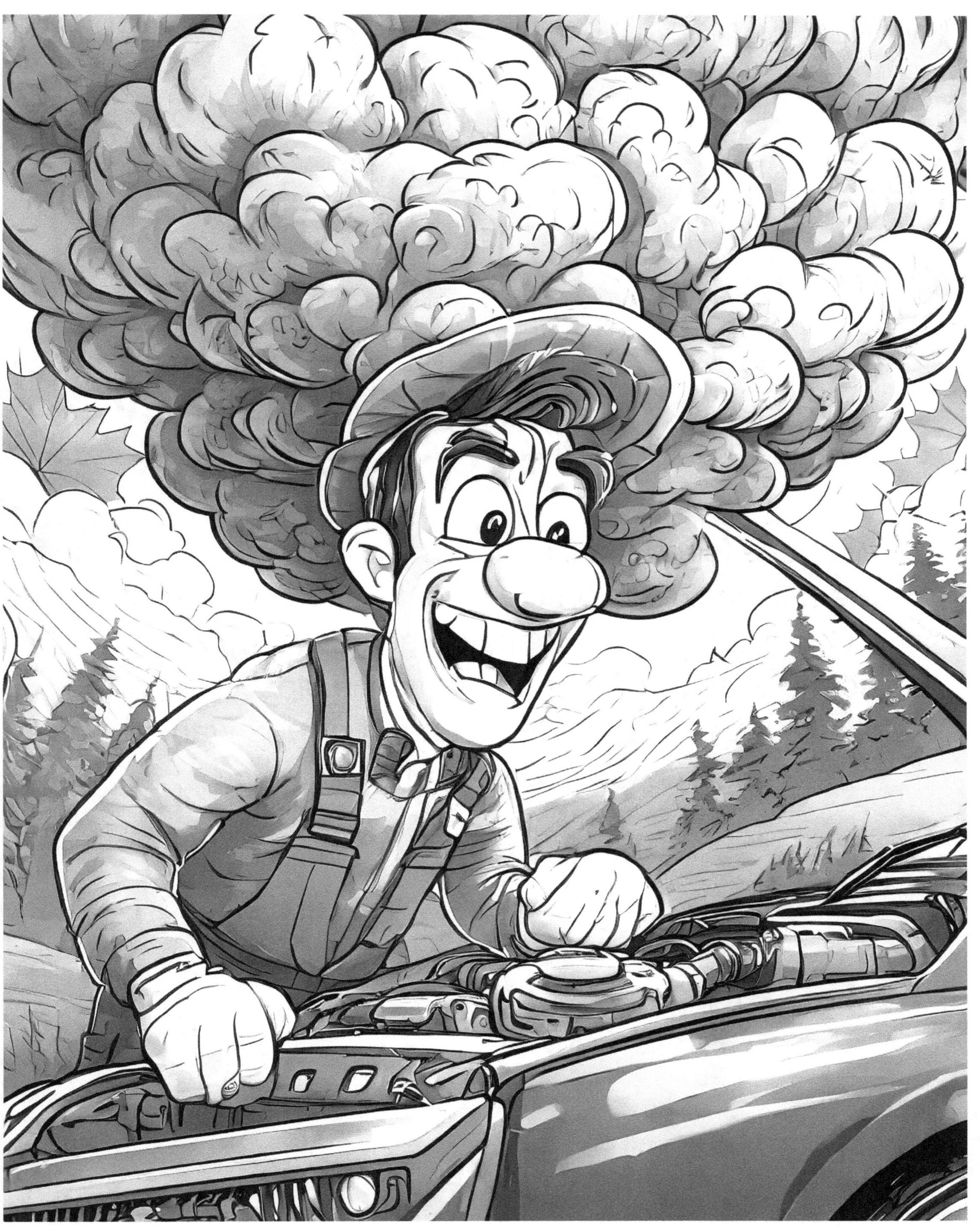

WATCHING HOCKEY ON TV AND FARTING?

If you have friends in Canada… Cancel your plans with them if Hockey is on the Tele. First off, it's illegal in Canada to miss "Hockey Night in Canada" and secondly, everything in the nation is closed anyways while it's broadcasting. You can fart all you want during a game, they won't notice anything.

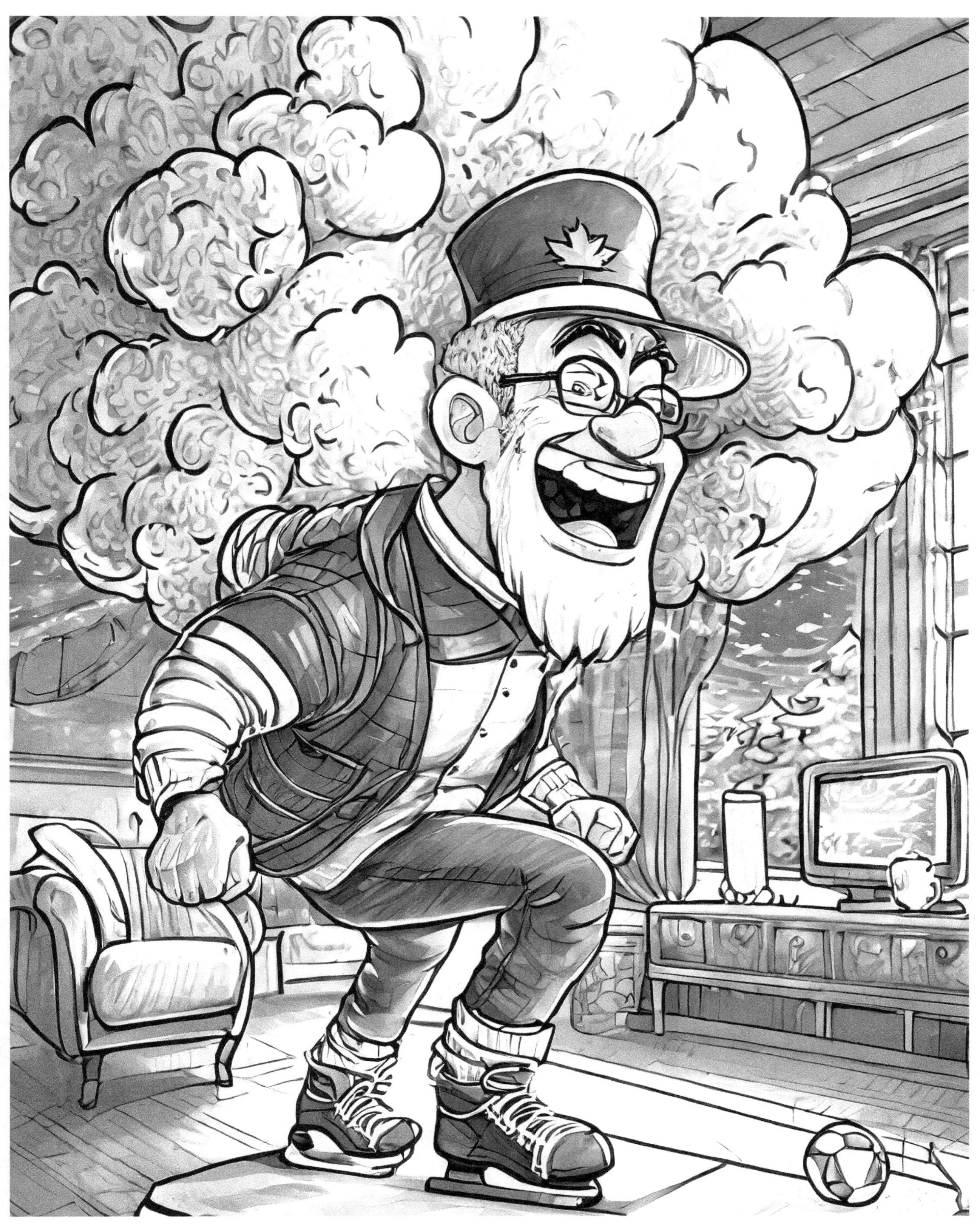

ICE FISHING FARTS!

Sit on some ice over a lake. You can find this at anytime during the year in Canada. Fart a few nice steamed dumplings and you'll have a hole. Put a fishing pole in the hole and wait… Drink beer and wait longer… Then… BAM! There's a fish. It's easy.

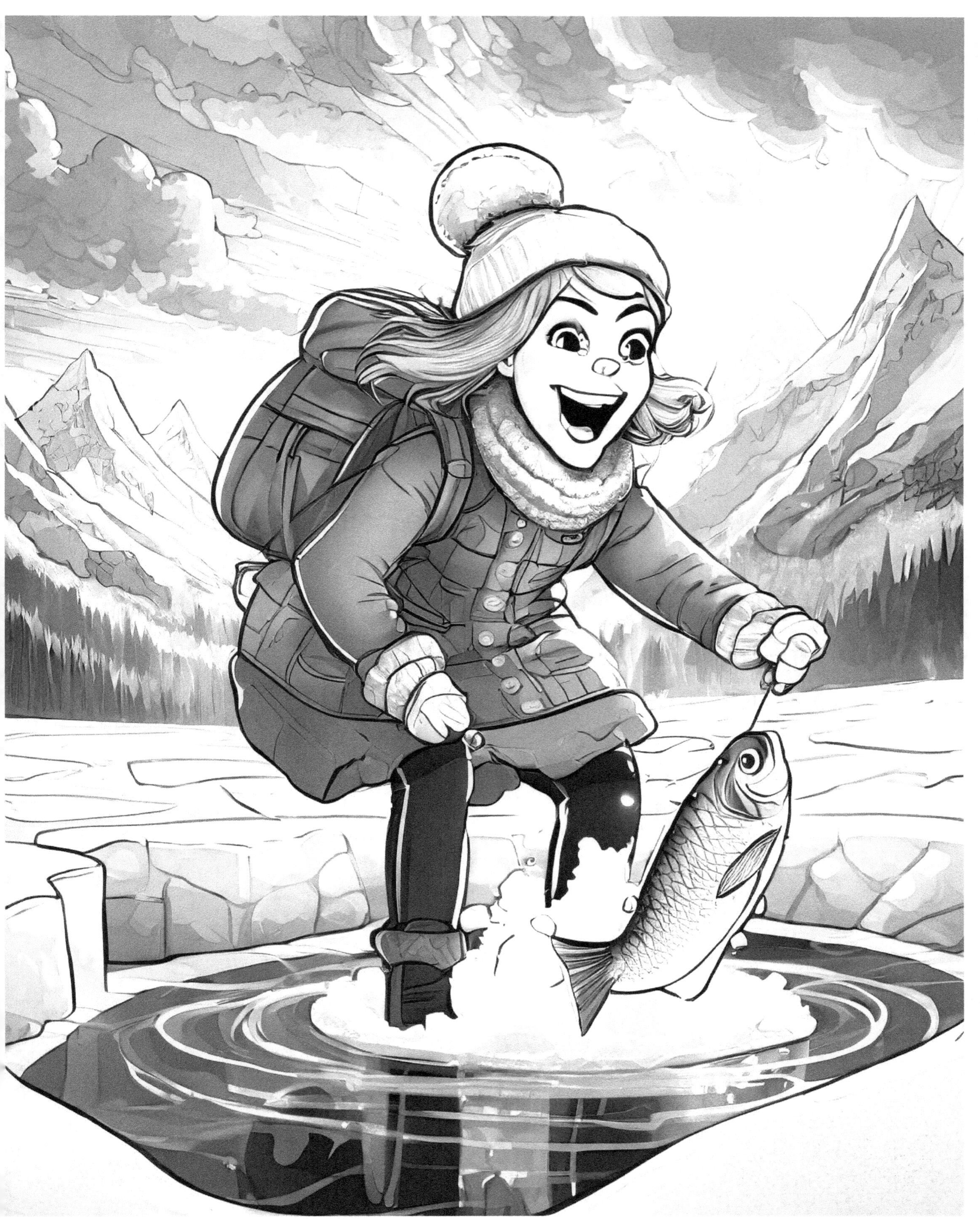

CURLING?

Sometimes you can fart and the paint on the walls will start curling, but I think this is a sport. Of course it's on ice and I think it's even in the Winter Olympics. Am I right here? You have to sweep or something as well. It's weird. And Canada has won the gold every year for 7 centuries. So yeah, Curling…

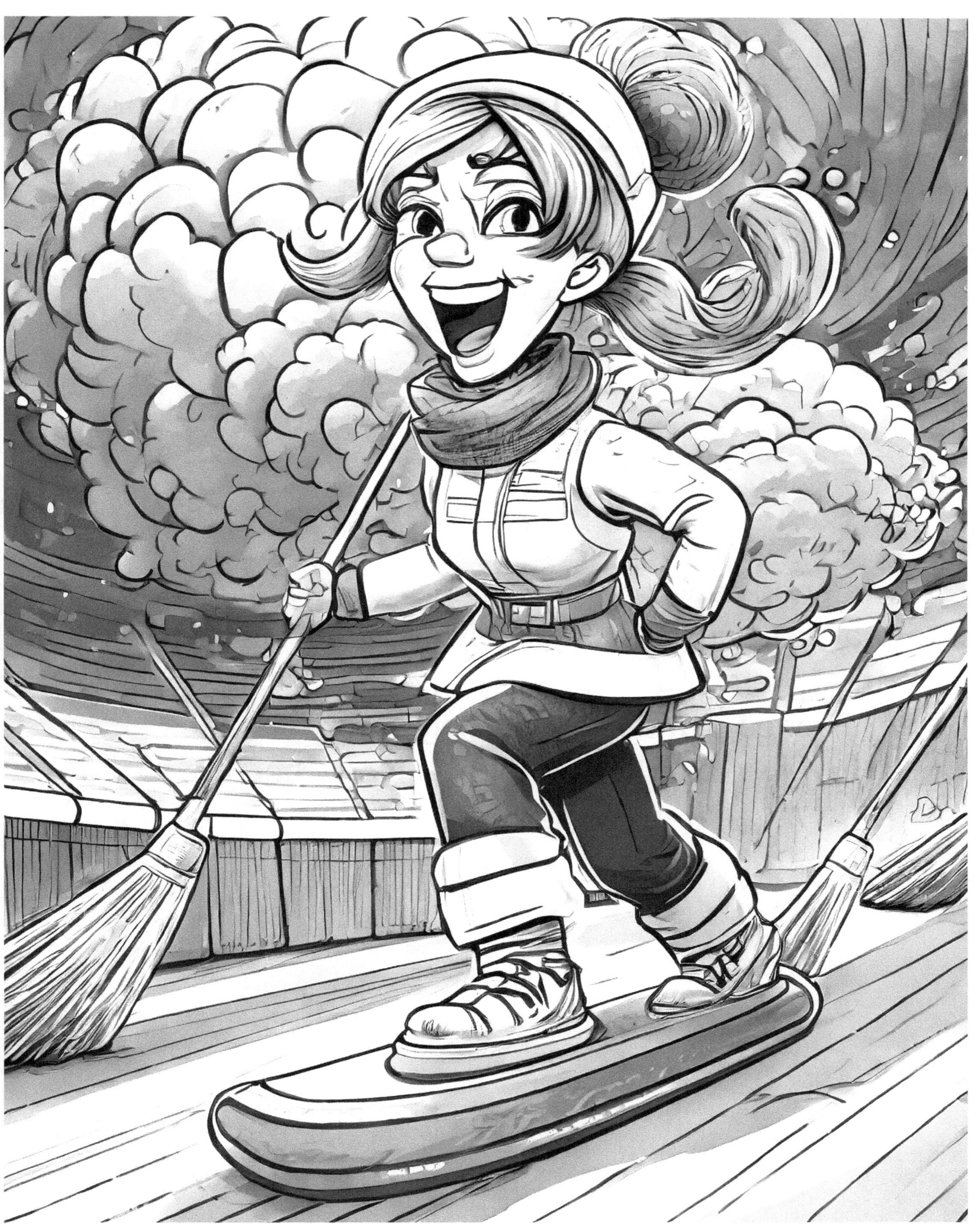

CANADIAN FLAGS ON EVERYTHING

As soon as you cross into the country you'll notice that the Canadian Flag in everywhere. It's also a law that there should be a flag every 17 inches. Small ones, but definitely a flag every 17 inches. On mountain tops… everywhere!

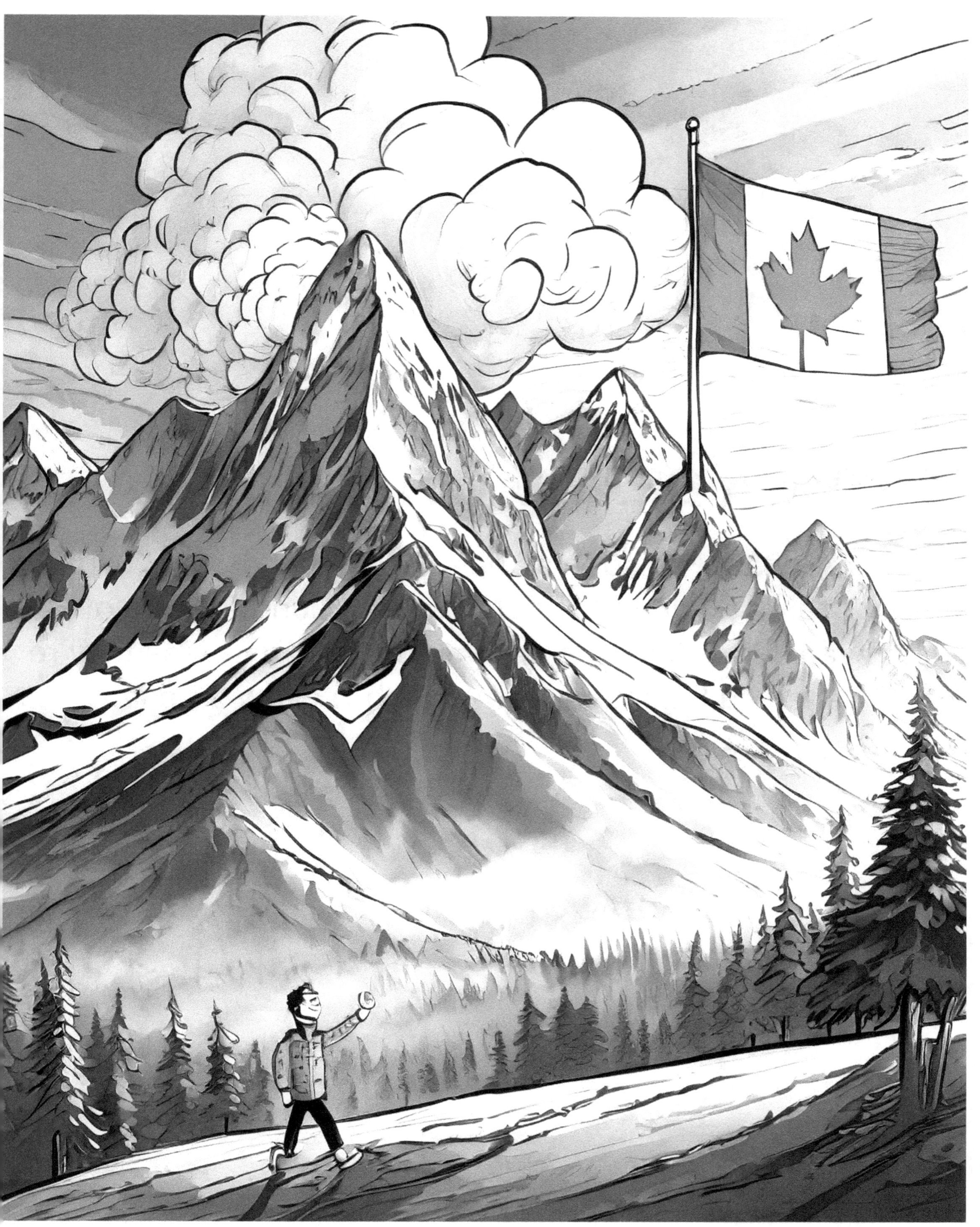

GROW A BEARD WITH THAT FART!

Men in Canada, as soon as hey fart on that moose, usually grow beards down to their stomachs around the age of 13. Not even science has an answer for this. Of course they're Canadian Scientists…so… yeah… Grow a beard!

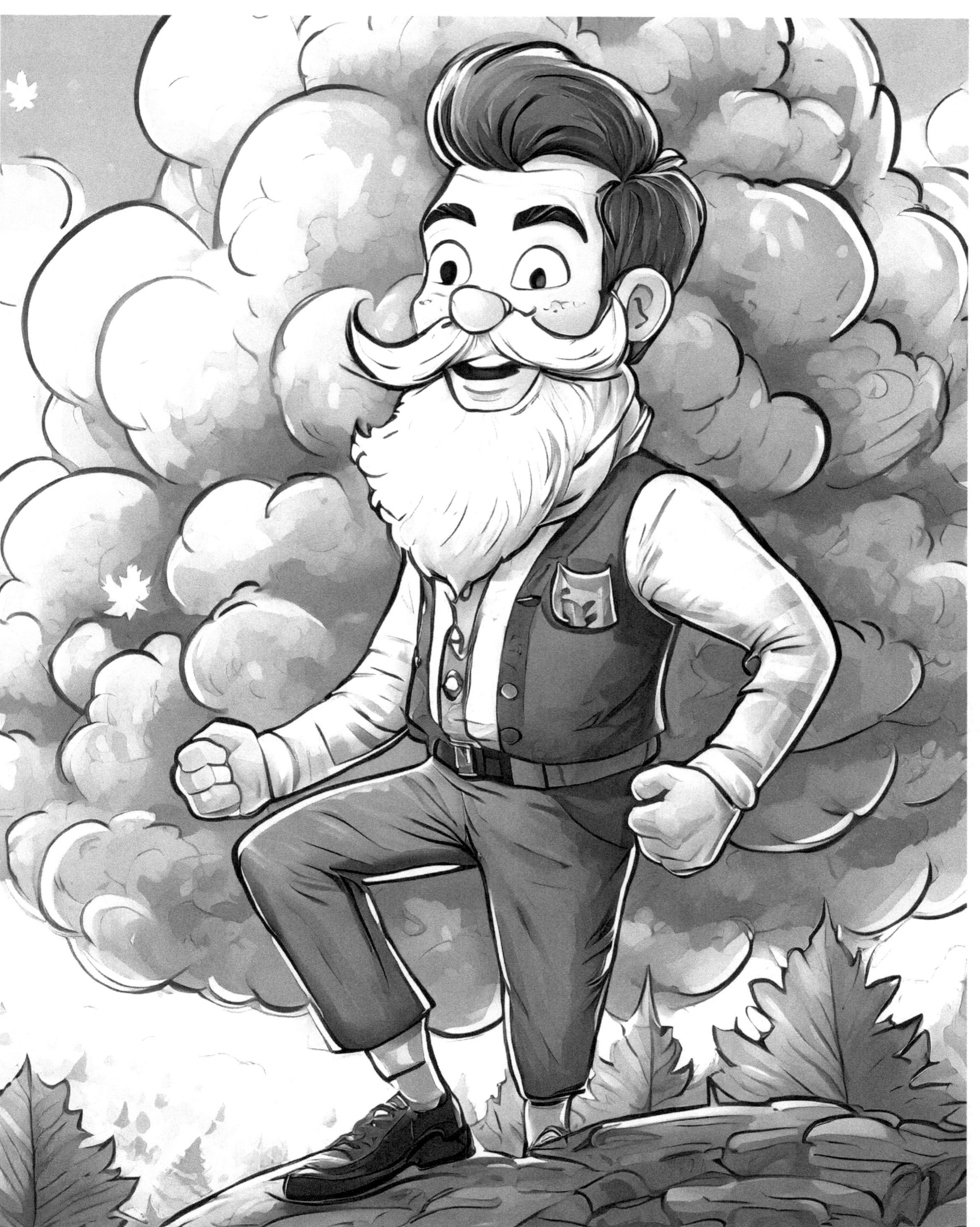

TOO NICE TO EVEN FART WHILE DRIVING?

Canadians are the most polite and respectful drivers on the planet. I really want to move there for this fact alone. They're so polite that they won't even let the gassy assy loose when driving alone.

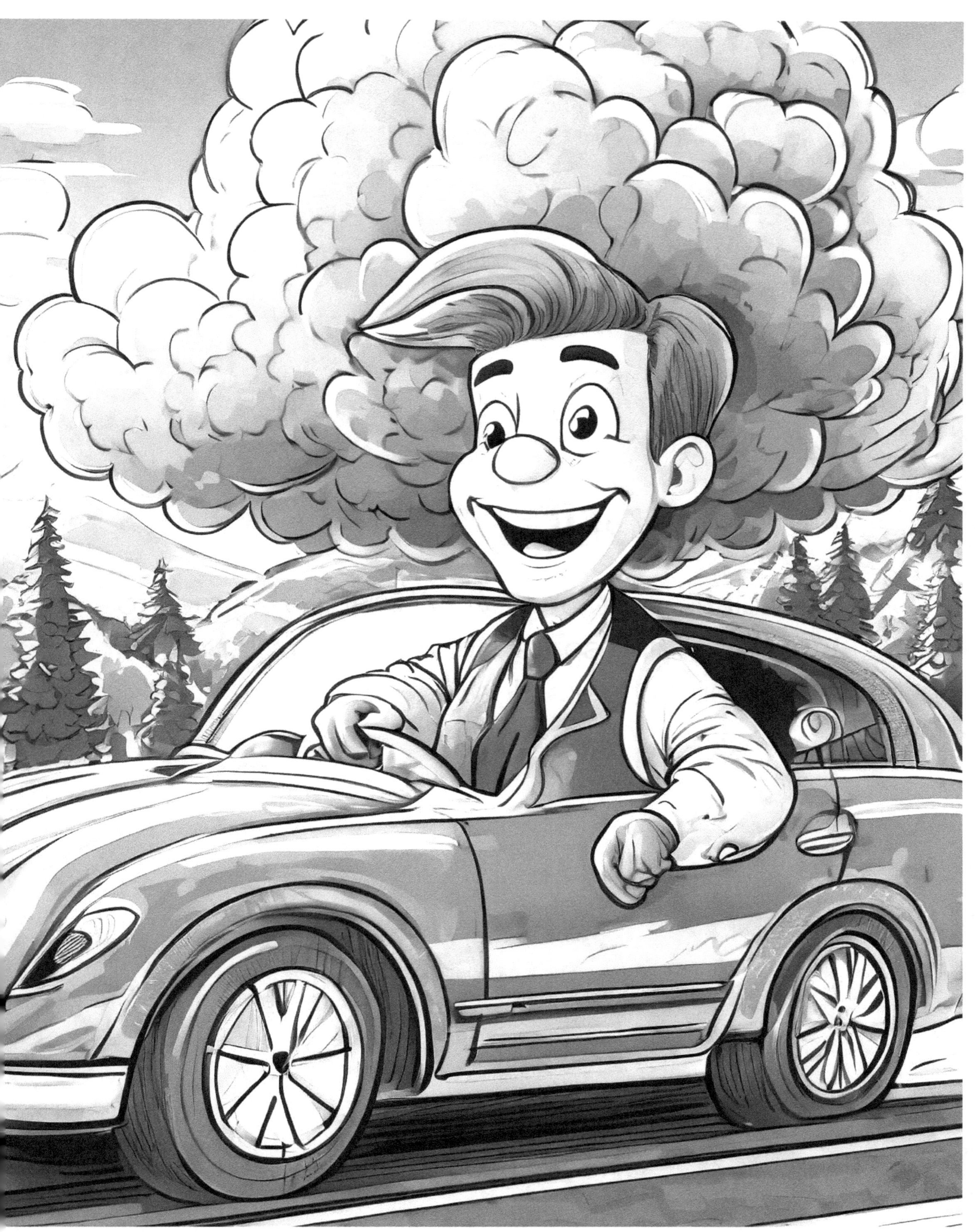

DUCT TAPE!

Canadians duct tape everything! Sometimes to avoid offending someone, they'll duct tape their butt cheeks closed. Proven fact.

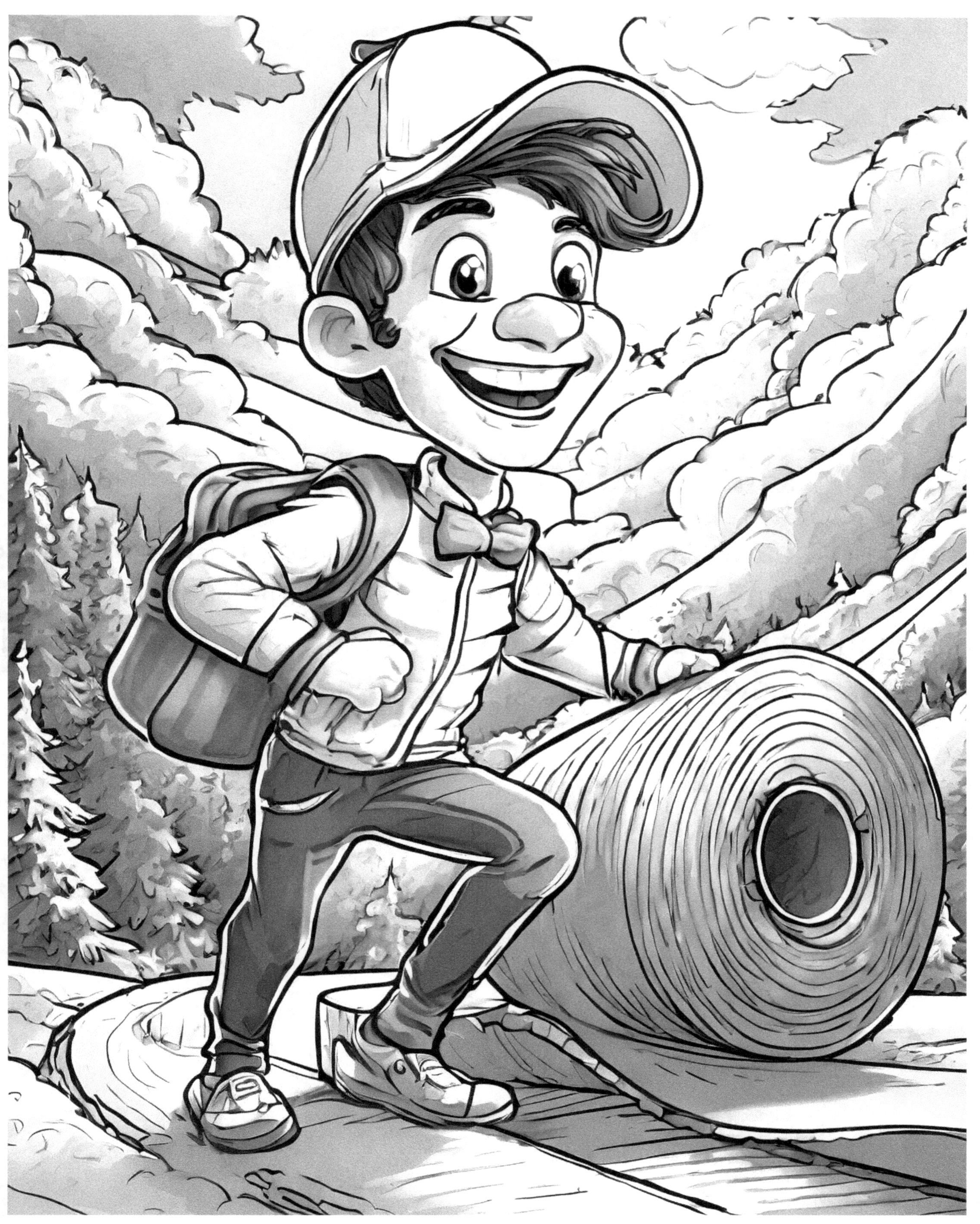

BEAVER TRAIL FARTS!

I have no idea what a Beaver Trail is and I'm far to lazy to look it up and learn. But Canadians spend about 1/4 of their life hiking these Beaver Trails and discovering new ones. I added beavers to the picture because why not?

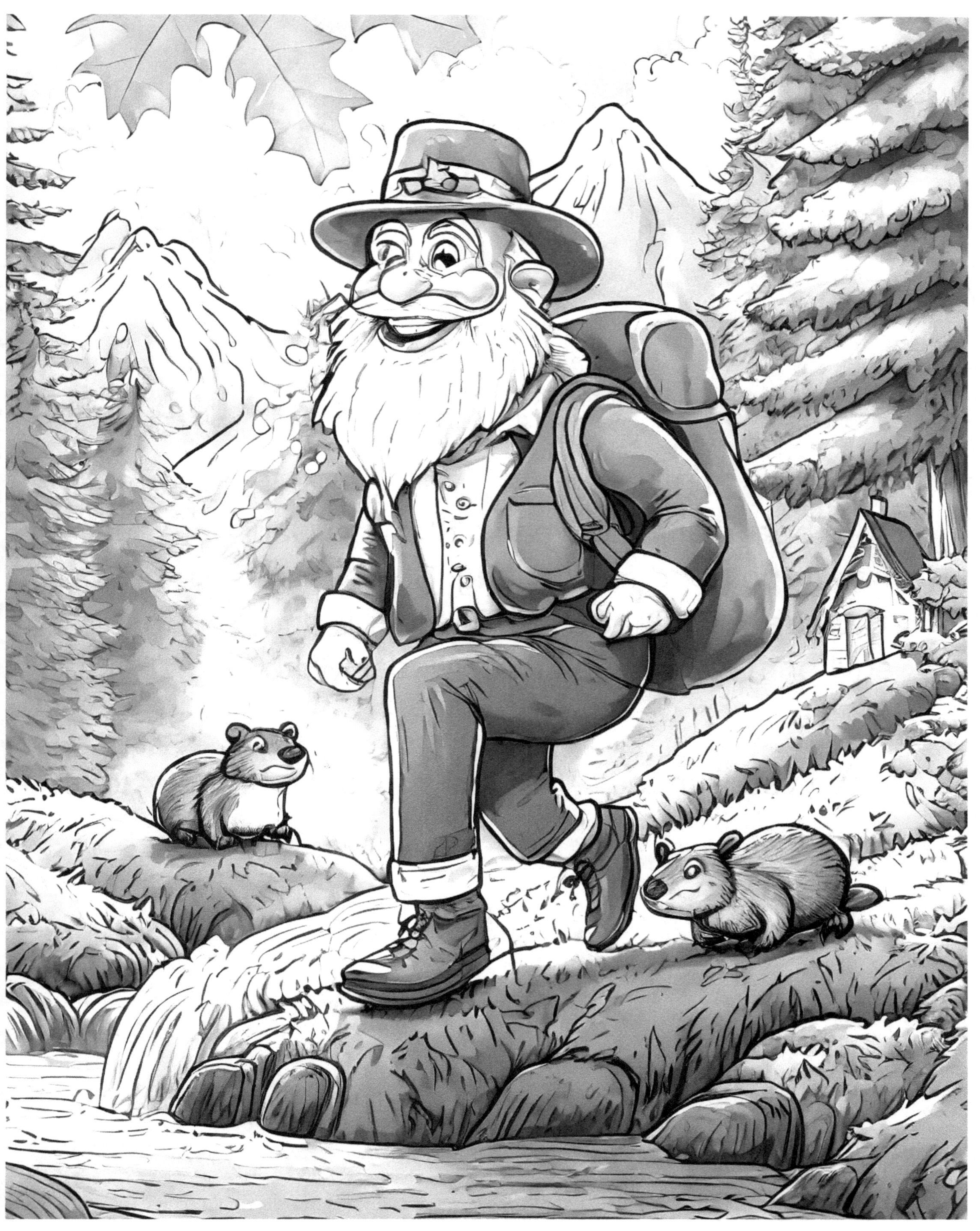

SHOUT OUT TO CANADA!

By SHOUT OUT I mean LET ONE OUT! That's right! No more beautiful fresh clean air for you Canada! You've had it too good for too long! So on your next trip to Canada, CRACK SOME THUNDER and pollute the environment with you Poo Winds! Make it smell like Texas up there!

We love you Canada! All of this was out of pure jealousy.

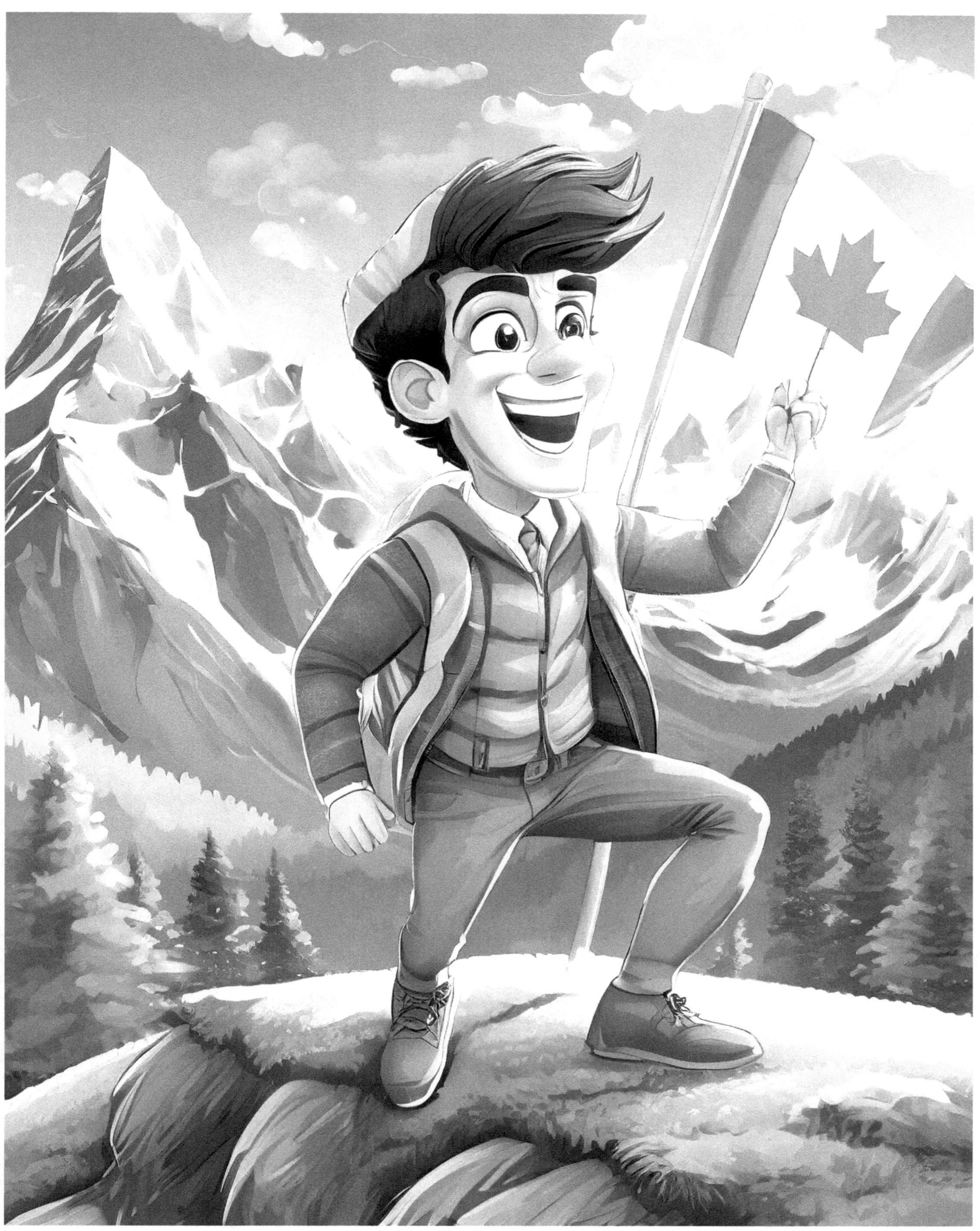

Where will we be farting next?

Let me give you a hint…

Tacos and Sombreros! Got it?

Go to our Facebook page and drop some suggestions!
Thanks for coloring! See you next time!

Written & Illustrated by Brandon Bishop

In Association with ASY TV

FANTASTIC PLACES TO FART
COLORING BOOKS

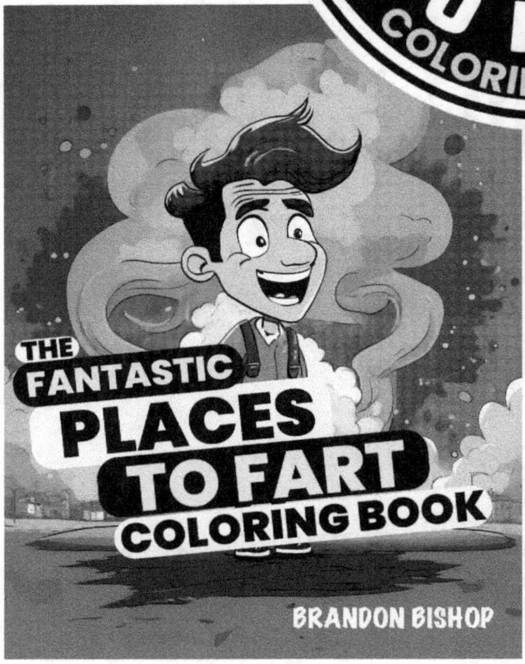

THE FANTASTIC PLACES TO FART COLORING BOOK
BRANDON BISHOP

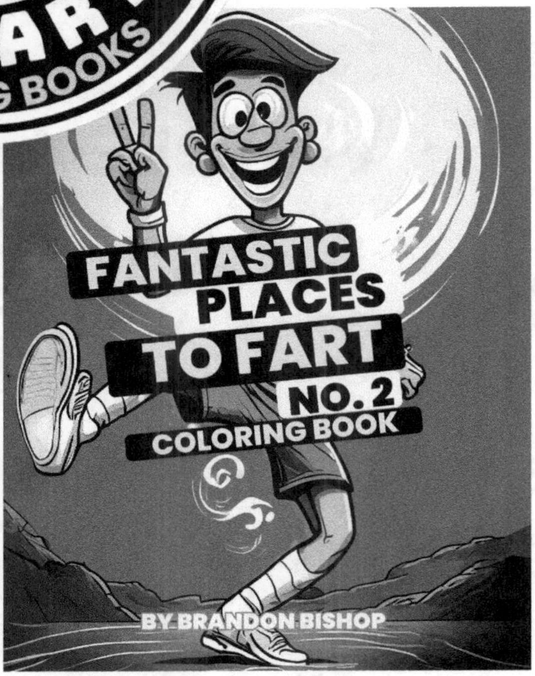

FANTASTIC PLACES TO FART NO. 2
COLORING BOOK
BY BRANDON BISHOP

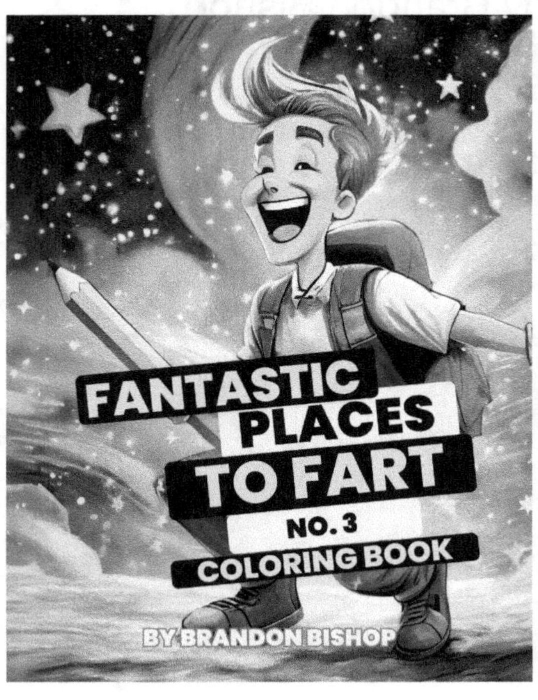

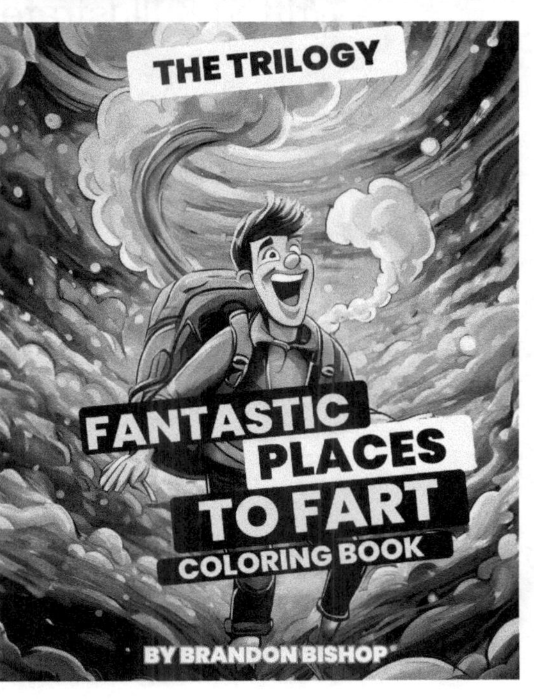

FANTASTIC PLACES TO FART
COLORING BOOKS

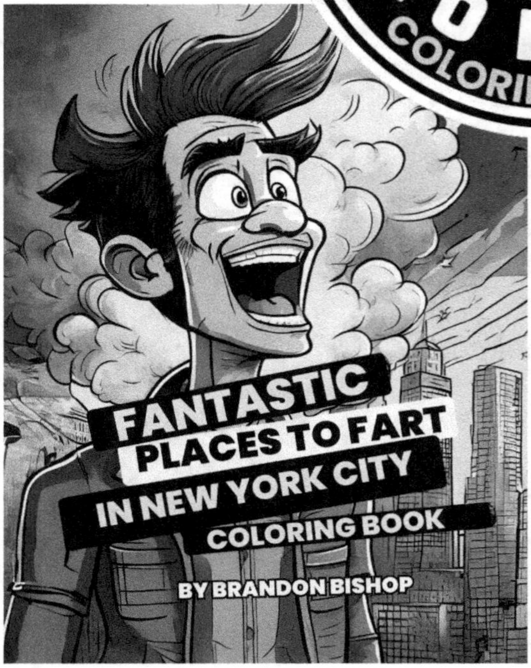

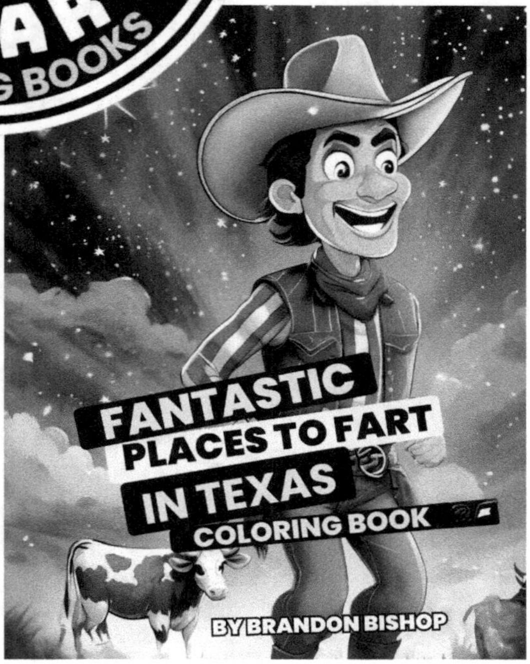

FANTASTIC PLACES TO FART IN NEW YORK CITY
COLORING BOOK
BY BRANDON BISHOP

FANTASTIC PLACES TO FART IN TEXAS
COLORING BOOK
BY BRANDON BISHOP

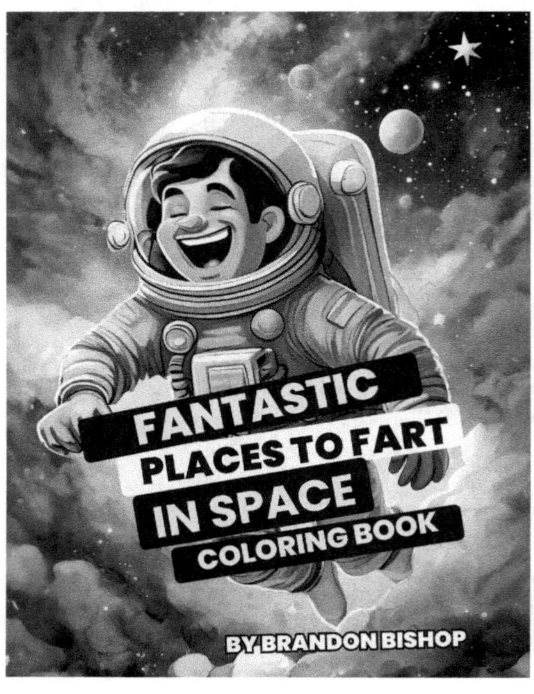

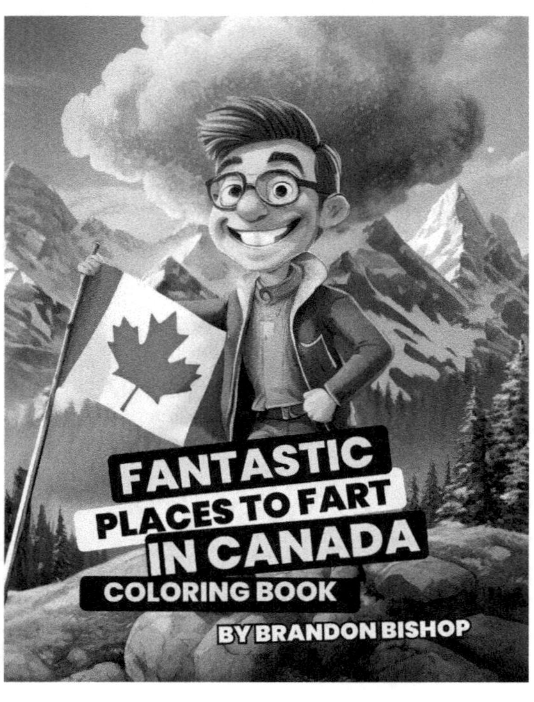

ANIMALS DOING HUMAN THINGS COLORING BOOKS

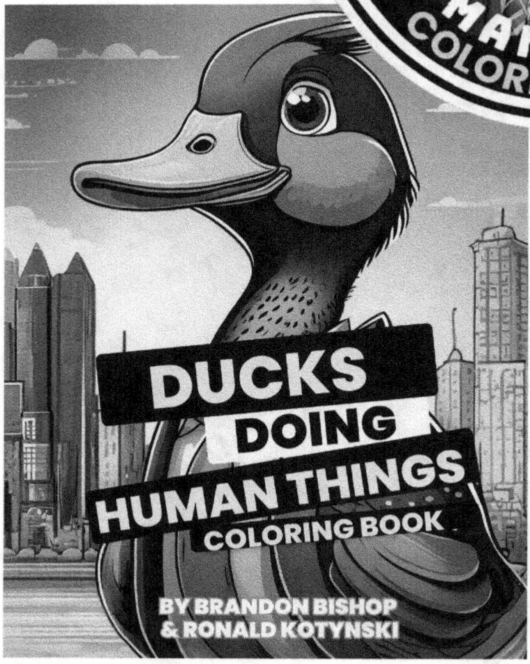

DUCKS DOING HUMAN THINGS COLORING BOOK

BY BRANDON BISHOP & RONALD KOTYNSKI

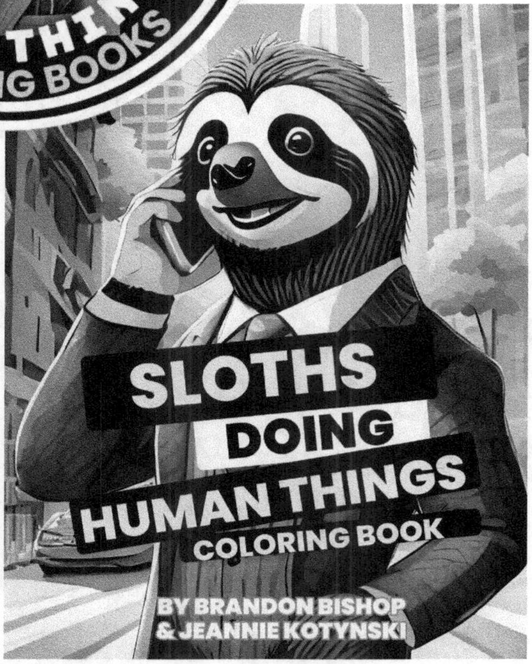

SLOTHS DOING HUMAN THINGS COLORING BOOK

BY BRANDON BISHOP & JEANNIE KOTYNSKI

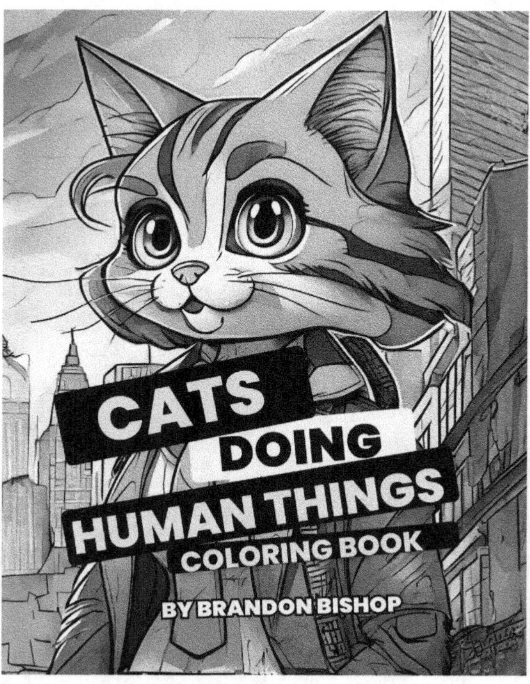

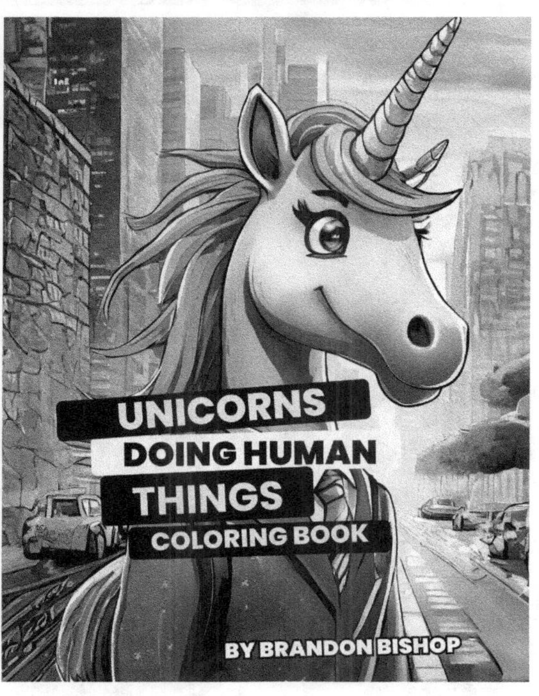

ANIMALS DOING HUMAN THINGS COLORING BOOKS

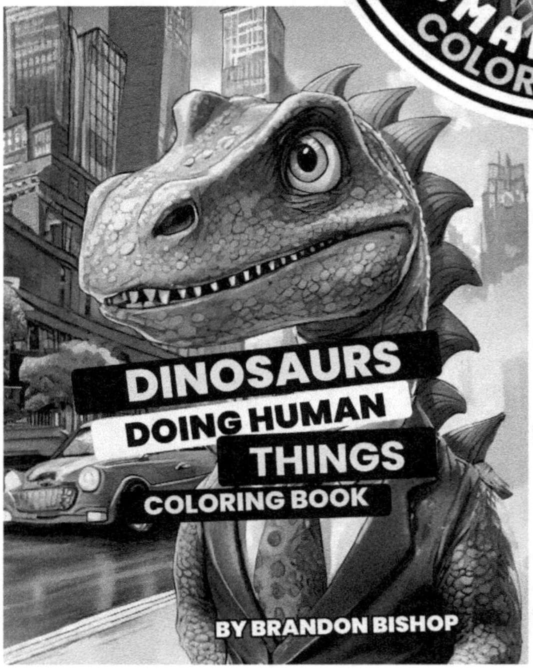

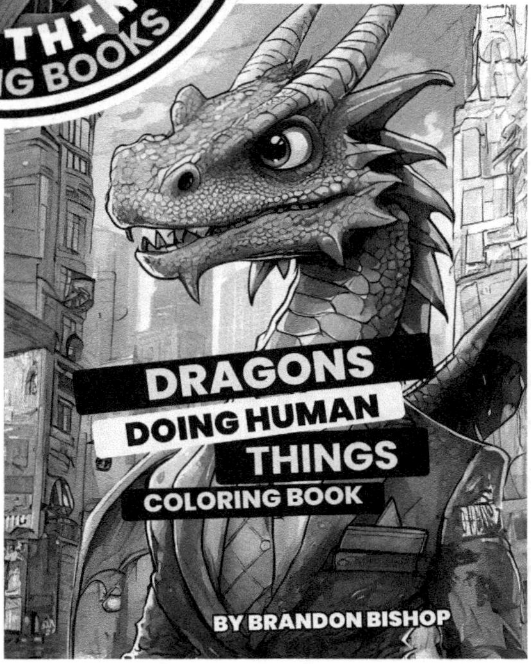

DINOSAURS DOING HUMAN THINGS COLORING BOOK

BY BRANDON BISHOP

DRAGONS DOING HUMAN THINGS COLORING BOOK

BY BRANDON BISHOP

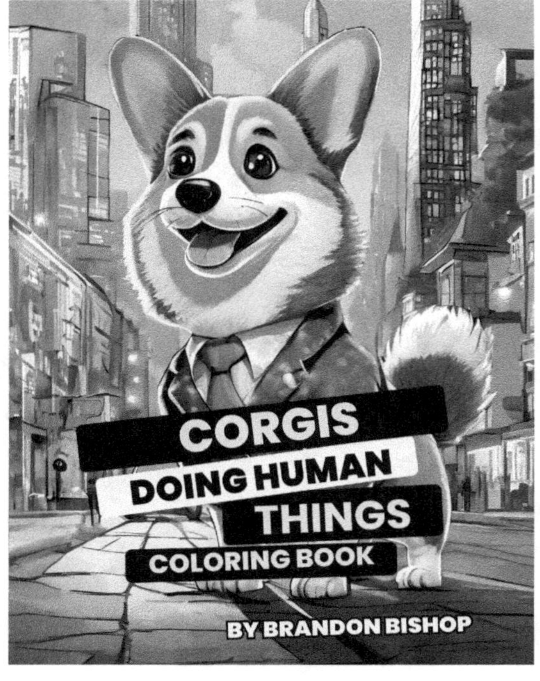

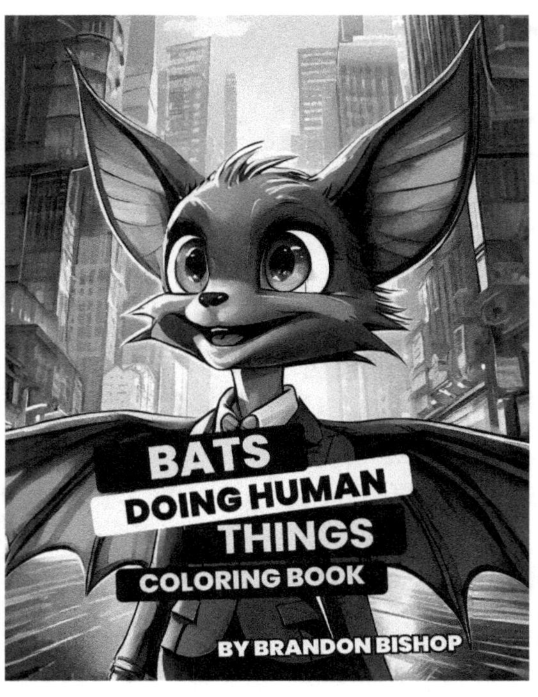

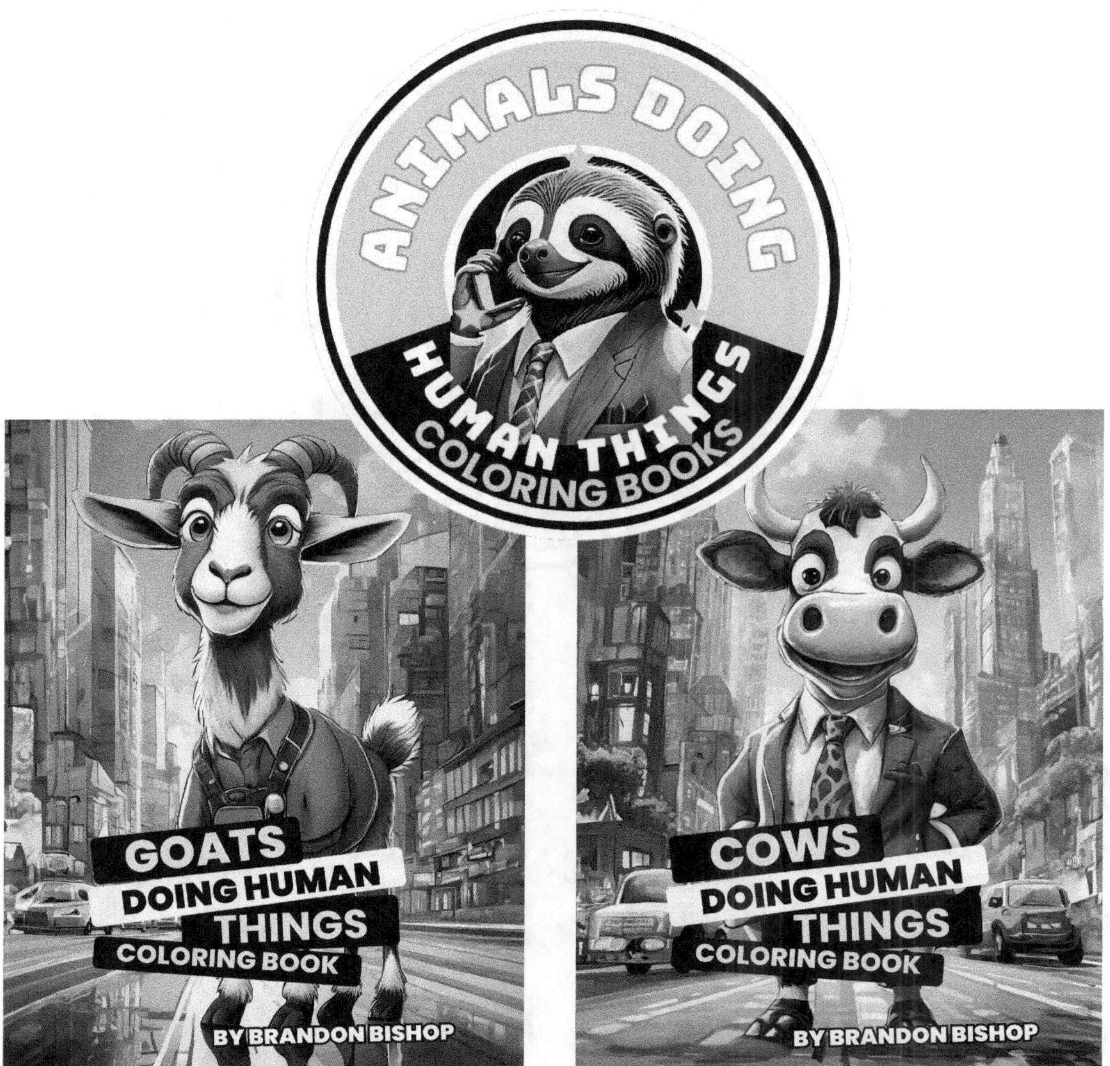
ANIMALS DOING
HUMAN THINGS
COLORING BOOKS
GOATS
DOING HUMAN
THINGS
COLORING BOOK
BY BRANDON BISHOP
COWS
DOING HUMAN
THINGS
COLORING BOOK
BY BRANDON BISHOP

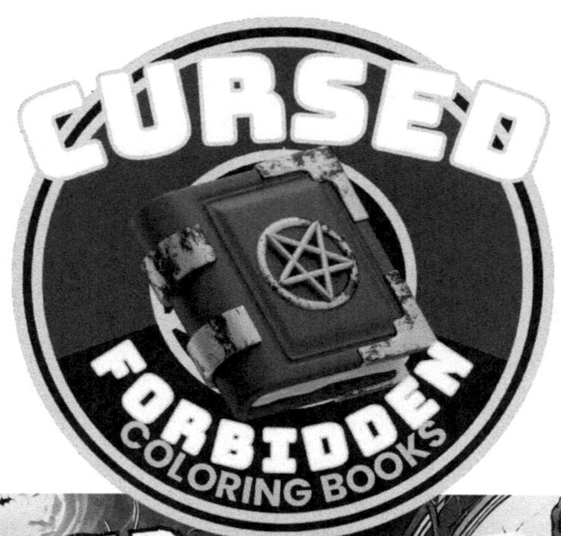

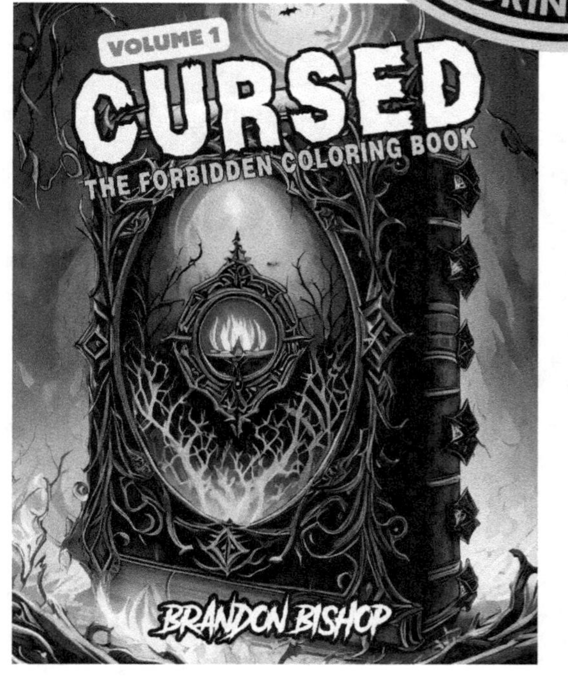

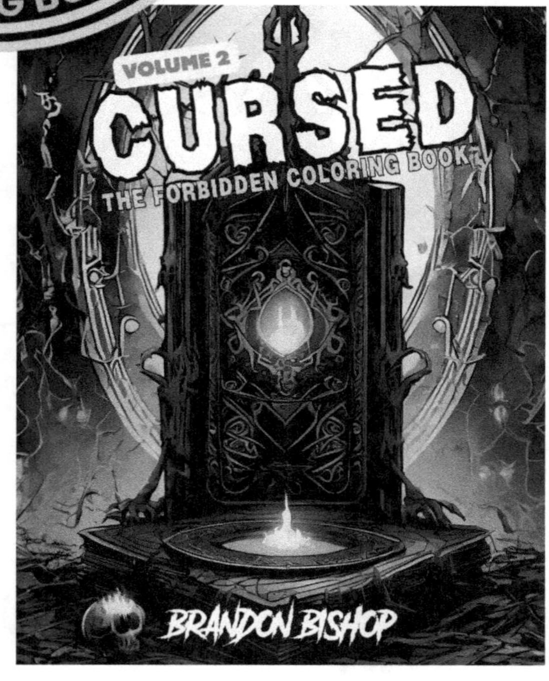

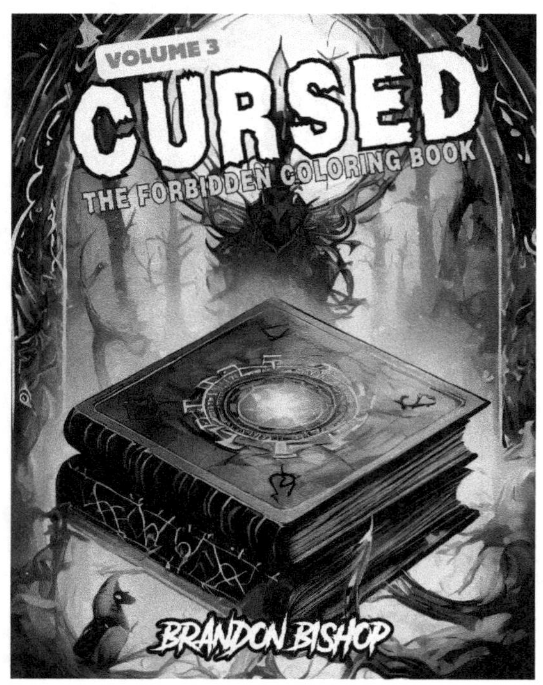

COLLECT THEM ALL!

www.ingramcontent.com/pod-product-compliance
Lightning Source LLC
LaVergne TN
LVHW080329110826
845155LV00026B/226